"Pastors Meador and Curtis have done a masterful job of exploring the what, the how, and the why of Christian stewardship. From the identity of the steward to the culture of the congregation, they provide a guidebook for pastors, congregational leaders, and members as they live out what it means to be a steward by God's design. I encourage pastors and leaders to read and study this important book together."

—Wayne J. Knolhoff,
former director of stewardship,
the Lutheran Church—Missouri Synod;
former director, the Center for Stewardship,
Concordia Seminary in St. Louis

"Pastors Nathan Meador and Heath R. Curtis provide a Christ-centered, pastoral guide to guiding souls from idolatry to joyful generosity. Through the school of hard knocks, faithfulness to Christ's word, pastoral care, and careful analysis, they have gained a wealth of wisdom. I've seen these men in action, winsomely teaching pastors and lay leaders, giving candid, down-to-earth, and road-tested insights into changing a congregation's stewardship culture. The book's conversational style and faithful teaching invites inexperienced and seasoned pastors and lay leaders to consider a plan that will strengthen and benefit the Lord's church for decades to come. I'm so thankful this wisdom is in print."

—David C. Fleming,
executive director for spiritual care,
DOXOLOGY: The Lutheran Center for
Spiritual Care and Counsel

"In this refreshing and delightful little book, two pastors shepherd us into the biblical world of stewardship. This is no pragmatic 'How to Raise Money' guide with a thinly veiled religious gilding. Nor is it an ivory tower theological essay void of down-to-earth advice. These pastors ground stewardship in our creation and redemption in Christ. They reveal its pastoral and congregational contours. And, with wit and wisdom, they map out the biblical path to stewardship that is in keeping with our life as the redeemed children of God, called to be stewards of his creation."

—Chad Bird,
scholar in residence, 1517

"*Stewardship: For the Care of Souls* is a wonderful book that will help pastors, church leaders, and individuals think wisely and biblically, rather than merely pragmatically, about the importance of stewardship in all aspects of our life, including but not limited to finances. Nathan Meador and Heath R. Curtis bring years of pastoral ministry experience to this project, weaving together theological commitments, biblical understanding, wisdom from their years of service, and insightful counsel for teaching and addressing these vitally important issues in the life of a congregation. This brief volume is another excellent contribution to the outstanding Lexham Ministry Guides. Heartily recommended!"

—David S. Dockery,
president, International Alliance for Christian
Education; Distinguished Professor of Theology,
Southwestern Seminary

"Every pastor should read this book. The engaging stories reveal how attention to the care of souls marks the pathway for creating a culture of faithful stewardship in your church."

—Gary G. Hoag,
president and CEO,
Global Trust Partners

"For the past twenty years there has been a growing movement toward recapturing the theology of the faithful steward for the body of Christ. Much of this work has focused on the para-church world. What has been missing is a winsome, robust, and biblically grounded resource specifically for pastors. Nathan Meador and Heath R. Curtis have now produced just such a resource. Written by seasoned pastors for pastors, *Stewardship: For the Care of Souls* is an absolute gem. You will find here a compelling call to rethink most everything you thought you knew about 'stewardship' and discover how God's gift of stewardship can transform your church culture and open your church up to be a place that truly preaches the fullness of the gospel. By viewing stewardship as pastoral care, Meador and Curtis have given us a fresh approach to this critical discipline of the church. I pray every pastor reads this book, and seminaries will include it in their curriculum. It is a treasure!"

—R. Scott Rodin,
president, The Steward's Journey;
author of *The Steward Leader,*
Stewards in the Kingdom, and
Steward Leader Meditations

"*Stewardship* isn't a sales pitch. Nor is it a step-by-step manual on 'how' to raise money. At its heart, *Stewardship* is about transformation. Nathan and Heath nail it. Finally, a thoughtful discussion focused on shepherding the hearts that make the decisions to fund churches and ministries all over the world. I strongly recommend considering the core message of this timely book."

—Brent Halvorsen,
church Generis strategist,
Generis Partners, LLC

"The cultural shift away from Christendom toward a more secular society makes it increasingly necessary for Christians to give an account of what they believe and how they live. This is true for all areas of Christian faith and life, including the way we think of such things as property and responsibility toward others. Rather than focusing on methods or results, Meador and Curtis consider why Christians think and talk about (much less practice) lives of stewardship. The answer they give is grounded in the biblical narrative and its description of a Creator who freely makes all things. He has made human beings in his own image and, through the gracious work of Jesus, remakes his people for participation in his work of caring for and restoring creation. This book provides a solid foundation for anyone who seeks to encourage a life of faithful stewardship."

—Peter H. Nafzger,
assistant professor of practical theology,
director of student life,
Concordia Seminary

"Nathan and Heath skillfully craft a refreshed perspective on stewardship. With soul care at its core, pastor shepherds discover how the whole counsel of God can enrich congregations in a stewardship-grounded identity that brings life and joy. Outflanking the usual pastoral chatter about giving techniques, this connection to stewardship as soul care will add depth, freedom, and joy to your pastoral passion. As a secondary win in this artful endeavor, your ministry will very likely be abundantly funded."

—Brad Leeper,
principal, Generis

"Here is a book worth reading, a refreshing perspective on stewardship. Anchored in the biblical theology of stewardship with a continued focus on the practical care of souls, Reverends Meador and Curtis use their own stewardship stories to draw the reader into a richer view of stewardship in the life of the Christian. The *why* of Christian stewardship remains the heart of center, entirely informing the *what* and *how*. There is plenty of practical application in these pages but not as you have experienced before. The pastoral art of teaching and preaching along with the culture that embodies a congregation's routine are challenged and pressed beyond simple program and useless cliché. Here is real meat for those hungry to engender in souls a theology of stewardship that sanctifies all of life."

—Bart Day,
president and CEO
Lutheran Church Extension Fund

"I appreciate the way Nathan and Heath approach the topic of stewardship—it's more about caring for the heart of the giver rather than about the money that is in their wallet. As spiritual leaders of the church, we need to help our people understand that it isn't what we want from them but for them. Changing the culture of stewardship takes intentionality and commitment. This book is a great foundational resource to begin moving forward toward the soul care of the giver."

—Sherri Adams,
Generis consultant and
executive director of stewardship and generosity,
Christ Church, Oak Brook, Illinois

"Stewardship is a subject few enjoy or even want to discuss. But Pastors Curtis and Meador not only discuss it, they seem to enjoy it. And you should too. The authors explore stewardship not as a necessary evil of church life but as a gift from God to his people. They help us think pastorally about our vocations and the duties of those vocations. They put stewardship into the pulpit before it enters the conference room. They know that the crucified and risen Jesus changes the way we see our God, our neighbors, our vocations, and yes, even our money."

—Rev. Todd Wilken,
host of Issues, Etc.

Stewardship

For the Care of Souls

LEXHAM MINISTRY GUIDES

Stewardship

For the Care of Souls

NATHAN MEADOR
& HEATH R. CURTIS

General Editor
Harold L. Senkbeil

LEXHAM PRESS

Stewardship: For the Care of Souls
Lexham Ministry Guides

Copyright 2021 Nathan Meador and Heath R. Curtis

Lexham Press, 1313 Commercial St., Bellingham, WA 98225
LexhamPress.com

Print ISBN 9781683594956
Digital ISBN 9781683594963
Library of Congress Control Number 2021930780

Lexham Editorial: Todd Hains, Andrew Sheffield, Abigail Salinger,
    Danielle Thevenaz
Cover Design: Joshua Hunt
Interior Design: Abigail Stocker
Typesetting: Danielle Thevenaz

For the saints of
St. John Lutheran Church in Plymouth, Wisconsin,
Trinity Lutheran Church in Worden, Illinois, and
Zion Lutheran Church in Carpenter, Illinois.

Contents

ACTS 20:28

Pay careful attention to yourselves and
to all the flock, in which the Holy Spirit
has made you overseers, to care
for the church of God,
which he obtained
with his own
blood.

Series Preface

Wʜᴀᴛ's ᴏʟᴅ ɪs ɴᴇᴡ ᴀɢᴀɪɴ.

The church in ages past has focused her mission through every changing era on one unchanging, Spirit-given task: the care of souls in Jesus' name. Christian clergy in every generation have devoted themselves to bringing Christ's gifts of forgiveness, life, and salvation to people by first bringing them to faith and then keeping them in the faith all life long.

These people—these blood-bought souls—are cared for just as a doctor cares for bodies. The first step is carefully observing the symptoms of distress, then diagnosing the ailment behind these symptoms. Only after careful observation and informed diagnosis can a physician of souls proceed—treating not the symptoms, but the underlying disease.

Attention and intention are essential for quality pastoral care. Pastors first attentively listen with Christ's ears and then intentionally speak with Christ's mouth. Soul care is a ministry of the Word; it is rooted in the conviction that God's word is efficacious—it does what it says (Isa 55:10–11).

This careful, care-filled pastoral work is more art than science. It's the practical wisdom of theology, rooted in focused study of God's word and informed by the example of generations past. It's an aptitude more than a skillset, developed through years of ministry experience and ongoing conversation with colleagues.

The challenges of our turbulent era are driving conscientious evangelists and pastors to return to the soul care tradition to find effective tools for contemporary ministry. (I describe this in depth in my book *The Care of Souls: Cultivating a Pastor's Heart*.) It's this collegial conversation that each author in this series engages—speaking from their own knowledge and experience. We want to learn from each other's insights to enrich the soul care tradition. How can we best address contemporary challenges with the timeless treasures of the word of God?

IN THE LEXHAM MINISTRY GUIDES YOU WILL meet new colleagues to enlarge and enrich your unique ministry to better serve the Savior's sheep and lambs with confidence. These men and women are in touch with people in different subcultures and settings, where they are daily engaged in learning the practical wisdom of the care of souls in real-life ministry settings just like yours. They will share their own personal insights and approaches to one of the myriad aspects of contemporary ministry.

Though their methods vary, they flow from one common conviction: all pastoral work is rooted in a pastoral habitus, or disposition. What every pastor does day after day is an expression of who the pastor is as a servant of Christ and a steward of God's mysteries (1 Cor 4:1).

Although the authors may come from theological traditions different than yours, you will find a wealth of strategies and tactics for practical ministry you can apply, informed by your own confession of the faith once delivered to the saints (Jude 1:3).

OUR LORD DOESN'T CALL US TO SUCCESS, AS IF the results were up to us: "Neither he who plants nor he who waters is anything, but only God who gives the growth" (1 Cor 3:7). No, our Lord asks us to be faithful laborers in the service of souls he has purchased with his own blood (Acts 20:28).

Nor does our Lord expect us to have all the answers: "I will give you a mouth and wisdom" (Luke 21:15). Jesus, the eternal Word of the Father, is the Answer who gives us words when we need them to give to our neighbors when they need them. After all, Jesus sees deeper into our hearts than we do; he knows what we need. He is the Wisdom of God in every generation (1 Cor 1:24).

But wisdom takes time. The Lord our God creates, redeems, and sanctifies merely by his words. He could give us success and answers now, but he usually doesn't. We learn over time through challenges and frustrations—even Jesus grew over time (Luke 2:52). The Lexham Ministry Guides offer practical wisdom for the church.

Since all things are sanctified by God's word and prayer (1 Tim 4:5), each volume in this series begins with prayer rooted in the word. We have Christ's command and promis : "Ask, and it shall be given to you" (Luke 11:9).

MY PRAYER IS THAT YOU GROW IN HUMBLE appreciation of the rare honor and responsibility that Christ Jesus bestowed on you in the power and presence of his Spirit: "As the Father has sent me, even so I am sending you" (John 20:21).

Father in heaven, as in every generation you send forth laborers to do your work and equip them by your word, so we pray that in this our time you will continue to send forth your Spirit by that word. Equip your servants with everything good that they may do your will, working in them that which is well pleasing in your sight. Through Jesus Christ our Lord. Amen.

Harold L. Senkbeil, General Editor
September 14, 2020
Holy Cross Day

Prayer for the Ministry of Stewardship

Since the earliest days of the church, Christians have used Holy Scripture to shape and inform their life of prayer. The structured prayer below invites pastors and laity to pray for the ministry of stewardship in the congregation. It can be used by either individuals or groups—in which case a designated leader begins, and the others speak the words in bold font.

In the name of the Father, Son, and Holy Spirit.
Amen.

O Lord, open my lips,
And my mouth will declare
your praise.   *Ps 51:15*

The earth is the Lord's and the fullness thereof,
the world and those who dwell therein,
for he has founded it upon the seas
and established it upon the rivers.   *Ps 24:1*
I praise you, for I am fearfully and wonderfully
    made.
Wonderful are your works;
    my soul knows it very well.   *Ps 139:14*
For we are his workmanship, created in Christ
    Jesus for good works,
which God prepared beforehand,
    that we should walk in them.   *Eph 2:10*

That God would bless his creatures to know the
    joy of bearing his image;
That he would equip his stewards to be his
    hands and his feet for the benefit of the
    neighbor;
That he would lead his stewards as they bear the
    gospel and as they use the gifts of creation for
    the sake of others;
Lord, in your mercy,
Hear our prayer.

That God would renew his stewards in the
    church to care for the world and those in it
    as he has cared for it in Jesus;
That he would enable his stewards to offer their
    bodies as living sacrifices transformed by his
    word;
That he would sanctify his stewards to carry out
    the priestly vocation for which they have
    been created and redeemed;
Lord, in your mercy,
Hear our prayer.

Our Father, who art in heaven,
Hallowed be thy name.
Thy kingdom come,
Thy will be done on earth as it is in heaven.
Give us this day our daily bread, and
Forgive us our trespasses as we forgive those
    who trespass against us,
And lead us not into temptation,
But deliver us from evil,
For thine is the kingdom, and the power, and
    the glory for ever and ever.
Amen.   *Matt 6:9–13*

Almighty God and Father, we are fearfully and wonderfully made in your image. Forgive us for our failed stewardship of that image in the world. Yet in mercy you sent your Son, our Savior Jesus Christ, to wear our flesh, bear our sins, and fulfill our stewardship. Clothed and called by him, lead us by your grace to bear the image of Christ to suffering souls in this broken world. Lead us to show your love to the unlovable, your faithfulness to the fallen, and your mercy to those who so desperately need your love, faithfulness, and mercy in their bodies and lives. Use our stewardship of the gospel to be an instrument in the hands of the Spirit so that others may see Jesus, the one who lives and reigns with you and the Holy Spirit, one God now and forever.

Amen.

The Lord Almighty direct our days and our deeds in his peace.

Amen.

CHAPTER 1

The Story of Stewardship

Nathan Meador and Heath R. Curtis

THIS IS YET ANOTHER BOOK ABOUT STEWARD-ship; however, this is not *just* another book on stewardship. Most books on stewardship focus on money management, the offering plate, and perhaps creation care. More rarely, works focus on the theology of stewardship. This stewardship book will be different.

It is not a book about the mechanics of stewardship from a programmatic approach. You will not discover in this work a tried-and-true, sure-fire method that will fill the coffers to overflowing so that the local congregation and the church at large can do whatever they desire in ministry.

Neither will the book simply give a paint-by-number plan to ensure the institutional survival of a congregation that has ministered for generations without ever adapting their approach to the world in which they have been placed for the service of the gospel.

What you will get in this book is a fresh focus on stewardship, with the ultimate aim being the care of souls.

This book focuses on individual stewards, their orientation toward God as stewards of creation made in the image of God (Gen 1:26–28), and their re-created image-bearing as stewards of the gospel of Jesus Christ, who endured the cross and grave to make his stewards new in time and in eternity.

This book will point pastors and steward leaders to the critical roles of preaching, teaching, and the pastoral care of stewards with the clear realization that poor stewardship is a matter not only of being stingy and miserly but also, in essence, of idolatry. The stewardship sin of idolatry, flowing from the first stewardship crisis of our first parents in the garden (Gen 3), highlights the need for the task of pastoral and lay leaders to preach and teach stewardship as a call to repentance and new life.

This book will present a practical theology of stewardship that calls both individual stewards and the congregation as corporate stewards to embrace and live in their identity as stewards who have been baptized into Christ.

This will come from the perspective of two pastors in the Lutheran Church—Missouri Synod (LCMS). We have unique stories that have led us to a common mission. One of us serves a larger congregation with a parochial school in Wisconsin. The other serves a small parish in southern Illinois just outside of St. Louis. We graduated from the same seminary about a decade apart. Our formation theologically, pastorally, and in stewardship was very similar. We have been led to a deep appreciation for the word of God and how it applies to the hearers entrusted to us.

We also share a rather spartan level of instruction in the area of stewardship. Yet, as often is the case, the Lord has led us to see that stewardship is central to the practice of the Christian life.

We pray that in our stories of learning and leading stewardship, you will discover a new stewardship story of your own flowing from the single greatest gift from God: Jesus. Individually and corporately, we have been created and redeemed to steward the gospel of Jesus Christ.

HEATH'S STORY: ONE OF NECESSITY

Right after seminary graduation, my (very pregnant) wife, our daughter, and I were bundled into the U-Haul with the help of her brother, and we headed north up I-55 to Chicagoland. My plan was more grad school and a part-time position at a large Lutheran church in the suburbs to help make ends meet. Grad school made sense because by nature I'm bookish: I still enjoy teaching Latin and Greek for an online high school as well as translating and editing seventeenth-century Latin dogmatics. (Yes, that's a thing. The publisher actually sells copies!)

Fast forward a year and a half, and my (again very pregnant) wife, daughter, son, and I were once again packing boxes for another move. Full-time grad school, part-time parish work, 2.5 kids in a two-bedroom apartment, an hour and a half of Chicago traffic every day—this was not working. I had dropped the grad program with a light heart, taught theology for a semester at an undergraduate college of our church, and waited for a call to full-time parish ministry. That call had come, and we were headed back south down I-55 to a dual-congregation parish in rural southern Illinois.

We loved it immediately. The people were wonderful, kind, generous, and truly supportive of the ministry. The parsonage was spacious and well cared for. The community was the All-American Great Place to Raise Kids. All of that was clear from the start. We moved in a week before Christmas, and as I write this, I'm sitting in the office in that parsonage having just celebrated Christmas here for the fifteenth time.

But just four months after that first Christmas, I got a phone call in my office. It was the president of the local bank. He said, "I just got off the phone with your head trustee, and he mentioned that you were new there." (He probably also mentioned that I was young and inexperienced.) "So I thought I would call you myself. I wanted to explain why we are going to have to cancel your congregation's line of credit."

Congregations had lines of credit? This was news to me.

It turns out that significant trouble had been brewing underneath the surface of this great congregation because for a number of years before my arrival, the congregation had been borrowing money to meet operating expenses for the church and school. If you have ever had to make payroll for a school or other business, you will know this fact of life: expenses keep mounting year in and year out. The congregation had originally started the line of credit as a solution to a cash flow problem; during the summer doldrums when attendance dropped and, thus, giving lagged, the line of credit would allow obligations to be met in a timely manner. Once fall came, the giving would go up, and the line of credit would be paid back to zero before the end of the year. This makes sense to a congregation with a farming tradition; it is how farmers can afford to put their crops in each year.

But you can see what happened. One year, the giving in the fall did not quite cover the outstanding amount with the bank. So the debt rolled over. It was just a little at first. But then the next year added a little more, and then a little more. Finally, it was too much for the bank to allow it to go on, and I got that phone call in my office that April. We no longer had the option of financing the parish and school budget with debt's revolving door.

What were we going to do? Closing the school was unthinkable. Paying the bills looked to be impossible. As Mr. Micawber says in *David Copperfield*, "Annual income twenty pounds, annual expenditure nineteen pounds nineteen and six, result happiness. Annual income twenty pounds, annual expenditure twenty pounds ought and six, result misery." We were firmly in the misery camp.

This was the crisis that forced me to rethink how our parish funded word and sacrament ministry and how I had been taught to instruct the people on matters pertaining to the law, the new obedience, and living out the Christian life. It forced me, a very bookish person, to dive into a real-world problem of ministry that didn't seem very theological at all.

I felt completely unprepared to face this challenge! Was it even the pastor's job to face it? I'm here for ministry, not fund-raising!

Throughout these pages, I'll return to my story to fill in the details of what has happened over the past fourteen years. But for now, let me make the long story short: we're still here.

A lot has changed: how we approach money, generosity, budgeting, and schooling, for example. A lot has remained the same: our theology, our love for the Lord and his kingdom, my love for the congregations, and their love for me and my family.

Back in those U-Haul-loading days, if you had asked me what aspect of ministry I might be writing a book about, stewardship would not have made the list of possibilities. It was forced on me by a crisis. But by the Lord's grace and a lot of help from faithful brothers in the ministry, the crisis led me to a greater depth of understanding, which made me a better pastor and my congregation a stronger and more faithful outpost in the Lord's kingdom.

Nathan's Story: One of Election

I have a confession to make. I did not come out of my mother's womb with a goal to become a steward leader in my local congregation or the LCMS. In fact, in my early formative years, I was not even a follower of Jesus.

Born in 1970 to a mother raised in the Roman Catholic tradition and a father raised in the American Baptist tradition, I was a child of the times. Mom did not want to be Baptist, and Dad did not want to be Roman Catholic. As a result, I spent the first years of my life without a home in either Christian tradition.

I likely would have stayed in this position had it not been for the single most formative moment in my life.

In September of 1975, my father decided he did not want to be my dad anymore. This shook my world to the core. My mother, reeling from the loss of her marriage, sought to reconnect with her Catholic faith. However, she had one problem: she was a divorced Catholic. This meant that she was not eligible for the sacrament. Making not much more than minimum wage selling jewelry at a downtown store, and having a mortgage and a car payment and three mouths to feed, Mom had no money available for the annulment process. This meant that she could not fully participate in the sacrament, which left her, and us, spiritually homeless. We were functionally unchurched for almost five years. That was when my stepfather entered the picture. He was a Lutheran.

At the time, he was what I have come to refer to as an *et ce*tera Lutheran. He was there on Easter, Thanksgiving, Christmas, and other random occasions. So while he himself was not the major influence in my stewardship journey, the Lord did use him to introduce me to three wonderful men: Louis Diepholz, Delmar Schoenleber, and Pastor Carl Aufdemberge. These three men saw something in me that no one else did.

Louis Diepholz was my stepfather's dad. He was a dump truck–driving blue-collar Lutheran layman who loved his Lord, his church, and his pastor. He served as a trustee, an elder, and the chairman of the building committee when our home congregation built its school. His good friend Delmar Schoenleber, a farmer short in stature but large in heart and service, taught the seventh- and eighth-grade Sunday school class for generations. These two men introduced me to Pastor Aufdemberge, one of those old-school German Lutheran pastors whom you loved and were terrified of all at the same time.

One spring Sunday morning in 1983, I arrived very early to serve as an acolyte for the morning's first service. Since I had time to spare and nowhere else to go, Pastor Aufdemberge invited me into his office. The dark-paneled room smelled of his stale cigarette smoke. The shades were drawn, and the only light came from a swing-arm desk lamp, by which he was reading over his sermon manuscript. It had the feel of 1940s film noir.

But then everything changed. He put down the manuscript, turned to me, and bluntly asked, "When do you leave for the seminary?"

Being thirteen years old and relatively new to the Lutheran Church, I answered quickly, "I am too young to die!"

He laughed and said, "No! Not cemetery. Seminary! I think you should be a pastor."

Later, I learned that Grandpa Diepholz and others had been praying for the same thing. Pastor Aufdemberge was ordering me into the ministry, and many others were praying me into it. I didn't have a chance!

Now, you may wonder how this relates to stewardship as the care of souls. On the surface, it does not. However, deeper down, it has everything to do with it.

You see, these men, who played such a great role in forming me into who I am today as a pastor, were almost always in lockstep with each other. In fact, the only time I ever remember them being at odds was over the topic of stewardship. The only time I ever remember Grandpa being upset at church was when the pastor was "preaching about money."

That happened on two occasions.

When I was a kid, November was always Stewardship Month. Preaching and teaching on stewardship always preceded the collection of pledges that would then be used as a planning tool for the budget that would be voted on in December. The only other time I ever heard about stewardship was when there was a shortage of money in the plate. Since our congregation had a school, that was often.

This formed my understanding, and my understandable fear, of stewardship. Every pastor has what I like to call his inner Sally Field. Years ago, when Field was accepting an Oscar, she quipped, "You like me! You really like me." No pastor wakes up in the morning looking for a way to anger people. Life in the parish is hard enough with all the brokenness that invades the lives of the saints, without adding their grumblings and complaints.

In my formation as a young Christian man, stewardship was one of those topics. I grew up thinking it was the third rail of pastoral practice: if you touch on it, you die! I was in the ministry ten years before I preached my first stewardship sermon, and that was only because the Lord has a sense of humor!

I am a convert to stewardship. My conversion was one of "election." While serving a congregation in southern Illinois, I was asked to allow my name to stand for election to our district's Board of Congregational Support.

There were four boards in our district. The Board of Directors handled all of the major issues. The Board of Pastoral Care was made up of pastors elected from each of our circuits as an extension of the Office of the District President. The Board of Mission focused on outreach in the district and internationally. The Board of Congregational Support was what I lovingly referred to as the "junk-drawer" board. It was tasked with everything that did not fit neatly into the work of the other three boards. Youth, schools, rural ministry, older adults, and stewardship were among the ministry areas in our drawer.[1]

At our first meeting I made a fateful mistake: I arrived late. When I arrived, the longtime executive of our district informed me that I had been elected "the stewardship guy." I did not know the first thing about stewardship. But I softened my opinion toward it because I learned that I would represent our district at the annual National District Stewardship Leaders Conference. I looked forward to it because it was in the Phoenix area in February, not because it was about stewardship; what a great break from winter!

God, however, had other things in mind.

He introduced me to men who had embraced stewardship in ways that I could never imagine. They gave me books that rocked my false understanding of stewardship and its practice. John Herrmann's 1951 book entitled *The Chief Steward*[2] and a pair of books by R. Scott Rodin, *Stewards in the Kingdom* and *Steward Leader*, were the introductory works that undid my false understanding of stewardship and led me to personal repentance over my fear of it. These great works caused me to see that stewardship is much more than just a necessary evil needed to pay the bills. Instead, it is a truly biblical practice rooted in creation and redemption. This truth meant that stewardship was an inherently theological task. This also meant that the pastor played a key role in the preaching and teaching of stewardship. As Herrmann and Rodin would make clear, the pastor is the steward leader. This rocked the world of a stewardship-averse preacher like me.

When you consider it this way, stewardship is something that must be taught. It must be taught because it goes against our nature.

We see this most clearly in the development of children. It does not take long to realize that children are inherently selfish and manipulative; they soon learn that if they cry, they get what they want. And while their first words are frequently relationship words—"da-da" and "ma-ma"—these words of identity quickly give way to words that assert their wills. "No!" and "Mine!"—a stewardship word!—become fast favorites (especially when younger siblings enter the picture).

The selfishness that drives poor stewardship is something we do not outgrow. The desire to claim ownership and control things are among the hallmarks of sinful human beings. And so the selflessness necessary for faithful stewardship goes against our nature and must be taught.

This means the faithful pastor and steward leader cannot avoid teaching and preaching on stewardship just because it might make hearers uncomfortable. Stewardship is part of the whole counsel of God. Just like pastors may have to preach and teach to address sins of adultery and theft and slander, they will have to call to repentance those who are locked into the sin of failed stewardship. Pastors cannot exercise a line-item veto, ignore the sin, and still view themselves as steward leaders being faithful to the task of pastor to which they have been called.

Repentance plays a key role in stewardship, and personally, the stewardship journey that began at my baptism has illustrated this reality. As I reflect on my own life as a sinner-steward, I see that I have often fallen short. The Lord has called me back to what he has created and called me to be. He has done the same for me as a pastor. I was not a faithful preacher and teacher of stewardship in the first decade of my ministry. I confess that freely. The Lord's radical generosity toward me in Jesus has restored me both as a child of God and as a pastor in Christ's church. Now I fully embrace the task of hearing and reading and teaching and preaching God's word in such a way that it leads those entrusted to my care, and perhaps you, to repentance and a new view of stewardship as a theological task that is much more than a chore or the cost of doing business.

The Story Continues

Our stories of development in stewardship are just that: ours. However, we are certain that for many pastors and steward leaders, there are elements to which you can relate. You may have been elected to a position of leadership for which you were wholly unequipped, like Pastor Meador was. Perhaps you were led by the Lord to serve in a position where the circumstances were dire and the easy route of funding via credit from the local bank, credit union, or extension fund was not an option, as was the case with Pastor Curtis. Perhaps you were the rare exception: you were served by faithful steward-leader pastors and parents who formed you for faithful care of souls to this day. Likely, your story is a mixture of all these stories. Your story might even be more fascinating than ours. However, it is certain that repentance is a key part of the process.

As you continue reading, however, you will see that the stewardship story is not a new story. It is not limited to the American church, with all the financial and societal pressures that beset her today. In fact, the story of stewardship begins where our Christian story begins. In the next chapter, we will begin with the *why* of Christian stewardship. From the primordial chaos of pre-creation, our Lord brought into existence a very good creation and entrusted it to Adam and Eve, the first stewards. However, under the pall of the stewardship crisis of the fall, we heirs of this stewardship task continue to be dragged down. Yet stewards today have been given a new creation in which we now live because of Jesus.

In view of this mercy, stewardship is not just an activity. It is an identity for which we have been created and redeemed.

CHAPTER 2

The Pastoral Care of Stewardship

Nathan Meador

NEITHER OF US WRITING THIS BOOK WENT from where we started to where we are now overnight. It was a journey. There have been many steps, and missteps, along the way. Moments of great development and growth have been interspersed with backslidings and failures. But as is the Lord's way, he has worked in mysterious ways his wonders to perform.

On the journey, we meet people along the way whom the Lord uses to move us deeper into our understanding of stewardship. For me, one of those people is Simon Sinek. While I have not met him personally, he has had a profound impact on the way I see stewardship as the care of souls. Sinek is not a theologian, but his understanding of leadership and inspiration have given me great direction. In his desire to help leaders inspire people to take action, Sinek points to the "golden circle," comprised of three concentric circles. At the center is *why*, the middle is *how*, and the outer ring is *what*. He argues that every company and organization knows what they do. Most companies and organizations know how they do what they do. But only the rarest companies know why they do what they do.[3]

Why is so difficult to define because it corresponds to the limbic system in our brains. The limbic brain is where our gut reactions are located. It is also the area whose processes we most often lack the ability to put into words.[4] It is the location of many of our most powerful drives to make decisions that often go against our rational, analytic thoughts.[5] When a business, organization, or, as I contend, individual steward can begin to put words to their *why*, they gain a better understanding of their purpose. When they understand *why*, the *how* and *what* flow naturally.

THE WHY OF STEWARDSHIP

Starting a journey from the right place is critical.

If I were to invite you to meet the wonderful people I serve in Plymouth, Wisconsin, I would be able to give you a tour of a beautiful and historic setting for parish ministry. I love giving tours! It is a testimony to the faith of the generations of pastors and laypeople who have been faithful stewards of the gospel of Jesus Christ on this corner of our little town since 1858. The sanctuary, constructed in 1890, and the building housing our day school, constructed in 1952, cover nearly three-quarters of a downtown block.

If, after the tour, I were to invite you to walk from the location where I serve to my home so that you could join my wife and me for dinner, I would give you very specific directions. Starting from outside my office, you would turn right, go so many blocks, turn left, and so on. However, if you followed those same directions but started from the opposite side of our campus, you would arrive not at my front door but instead rather close to the entrance of one of the seedier taverns in my town. You can get a good burger and a beer there, but you will pay for it!

Journeys, even with good directions, must begin in the right place. This is true of walking the streets of Plymouth, Wisconsin, and it is also true of the stewardship journey that pastors and those under their care are on.

For the last three decades, my denomination has defined stewardship this way: "Christian stewardship is the free and joyous activity of the child of God and God's family, the church, in managing all of life and life's resources for God's purposes."[6] It has served our church well. Yet this definition makes an often-committed mistake in teaching stewardship. It focuses on the *what* and *how* of stewardship, without capturing the *why*.

When we become fixated on stewardship's *what* and *how*, we are starting in the wrong place. When a pastor teaches tithing and offerings, percentage giving, sacrificial service, and many other concepts of the *what* and *how* of stewardship, without providing the stewards with a clear view of the *why*, the stewards end up lost. St. Paul talks to the Corinthians about how much God loves a cheerful giver, but without knowing the *why* of stewardship, cheerfulness is not possible. People may faithfully give and serve, but what they have lost is the freedom and joy of knowing why they are stewards in the first place.

CREATED FOR STEWARDSHIP

To capture the *why* of stewardship, stewards must be taught their identity before they are taught their activity. To find this identity, look no further than Genesis 1:26–28.

> Then God said, "Let us make man in our image, after our likeness. And let them have dominion over the fish of the sea and over the birds of the heavens and over the livestock and over all the earth and over every creeping thing that creeps on the earth." So God created man in his own image, in the image of God he created him; male and female he created them. And God blessed them. And God said to them, "Be fruitful and multiply and fill the earth and subdue it, and have dominion over the fish of the sea and over the birds of the heavens and over every living thing that moves on the earth."

Our identity as stewards is rooted in the Lord's created order. The modern church very often defines the vocation of steward by its activity. Our sinful human nature hears instructions like "have dominion" and "subdue" and receives them with great glee. Who would not want to have dominion over all creation? In the fallen mind, it is good to be king. When people think they are kings, calling the shots is seen as a benefit.

Here again it is necessary to start at the right place: with the creation of the stewards in the "image of God." The Hebrew word used here, which occurs only four times in the Hebrew Scriptures, all of which are in Genesis, connotes an image or reflection of the original.[7] This means that the activity of stewards, subduing and having dominion, is modified by the identity for which stewards have been created. Stewards are to carry out the stewardship of subduing and having dominion as a reflection of the Creator. Stewards are not tyrants to domineer over creation or to beat it into submission to their will. Stewards are to reflect the will and heart of the Owner of all things, who by virtue of creation is God. So all of creation, including humans as its stewards, is to be an extension of the heart of the Creator. Within this image, the holy and just steward is to do exactly what the Lord created him to do: steward creation.

This identity is then further clarified in the next chapter of Genesis. Here, stewards are given a very clear purpose: "The LORD God took the man and put him in the garden of Eden to work it and keep it" (Gen 2:15). The man was created for the task of work. Work is regarded as an essential part of the human existence. Human beings cannot have meaning or fulfillment without this obligation.[8] The labor that is stewardship was a joyful labor. At this point, stewardship was not a chore or a bore. It was exactly what humanity was created for.

Stewardship is a priestly task. The Hebrew in this passage makes this clear. While the words for work (*avad*) and keep (*shamar*) are common in the Old Testament, they both have priestly overtones. *Avad* describes the priests' work in the temple; *shamar* describes the priests' task of defending the temple. Work and worship go together.[9] St. Paul echoes this in Romans 12. Human work is human worship of God. In our working and keeping of creation, we do what the Lord has given us to do.

This is the *why* of stewardship. God has made us for this purpose![10] There was only one vocation in the garden: that of steward. Like a hammer was created to drive a nail, people were created by God to serve as stewards. The purpose of stewardship does not begin with us. It begins in the creative power of God. He is the one who conceived this role. It is not an act of volunteerism or generosity. When stewards manage all of life and life's resources for God's purposes, they are simply doing what they have been given to do. Only when there is synchronicity between identity and activity, purpose is realized, and joy ensues. We will never find this if we start our stewardship journey from the point of what stewards do. When we embrace our identity as stewards, reflecting God's image by the way we manage creation for God's glory and the benefit of our neighbor, we are starting with our *why*. This aligns God's word and our purpose and allows for the golden circle of stewardship to radiate from God, through us, to others. Stewards were made for this!

Stewardship Crisis

As Genesis 2 closes, we find a perfect creation, declared by God to be very good, entrusted to perfect stewards to be managed as a reflection of God's will in creation. The tripartite relationship among Creator, steward, and creation was exactly the way it had been designed. How long did this last? Well, in most personal copies of the Holy Scriptures, it lasts about a page turn. That page turn is devastating. The page turn, however, is not the problem. What takes place with the turn of the page is the turn of the hearts of the perfectly naked and shameless stewards. Our exegetical friends will call Genesis 3 the fall into sin. That assertion is antiseptic and scholarly. It misses a serious point. What takes place in the exchange of Genesis 3 is really more rightly called the first stewardship crisis.

We know the story well. Adam and Eve were doing what God had created them to do. They were embracing their *why*. But entering the scene is a new, tainted character. Slithering up to the woman in the midst of her stewardship, the ancient serpent opens a disastrous dialogue. Skipping the small talk, the serpent begins the process of getting the fully blessed stewards to start thinking that God is holding out on them. Remember, Eve confesses that they could eat anything else in the garden except for the fruit of the tree in the center of the garden. One tree out of the whole universe was off limits! This sounds like such an easy temptation to overcome. As the text clearly indicates, it is a test that our first parents fail at miserably. Being tempted with a new voice and a twisted message, Eve begins looking at things differently. With seeing things the serpent's way comes covetousness. We see that play out in the most devastating of ways.

> So when the woman saw that the tree was good for food, and that it was a delight to the eyes, and that the tree was to be desired to make one wise, she took of its fruit and ate, and she also gave some to her husband who was with her, and he ate. Then the eyes of both were opened, and they knew that they were naked. (Gen 3:6–7)

What takes place in these familiar yet profoundly destructive words is failed stewardship. This failure marks the beginning of death. The consequence is best illustrated in the position of the stewards' hands. Prior to this devastating stewardship crisis, the hands of the first stewards were outstretched toward God. Everything in creation had been designed by God to come as a blessing. While the first stewards were to cultivate the creation, it was really a matter of simply harvesting what the creation naturally provided. As the cited verses indicate, the covetous look soon leads to a destructive change of hand position. The woman, her perspective twisted by the false words of the serpent, reaches out, not to receive but to take.

The taking, the reaching out for what was forbidden, is the point of no return. The overturned hand, no longer receiving but taking, marks the tipping point where the stewards' activity betrays their identity. As the hand rolls over, reaches, grasps, takes, eats, and gives, the transition from steward to presumed owner is complete; however, there has been no transfer of ownership. The Creator has not given deed and title of any of creation to the stewards. The stewards simply and boldly assert ownership over something that is not rightfully theirs. We have a word for this action: theft.

There is a theft in God's perfect garden. But the theft of the fruit is the symptom of a much greater, more damaging theft. In the seeing, reaching, taking, eating, and sharing, the stewards assert their will over God's. The theft is ultimately of God's place. The created stewards attempt to become the Creator. This seriously raises the staggering impact of failed stewardship. It is not a matter of stinginess or miserly behavior. Failed stewardship is, at its heart, idolatry! The failure to keep the only command in the garden is the manifestation of the sin against the first commandment. The stewards want to be God.

The creature cannot be the Creator. The steward cannot be the Owner. To attempt to steal this place and redefine this relationship has devastating consequences. The perfect relationship between Creator, steward, and creation is shattered. As God walks in the garden, the open-eyed stewards realize their nakedness and shame. When they are confronted with their idolatrous theft, the blame game ensues. The man blames the woman and, eventually, God himself. The woman blames the serpent. The serpent is without excuse.

As the judgment falls upon all creation because of the duplicity of the stewards, the creation, which had been designed to support the stewards' life, will now cause them pain and eventually be the death of them. All of life prior to the stewardship crisis was always work. But the work is now hard. The fallout of this stewardship crisis is toil. Sweat, suffering, pain, and problems become the hallmarks of stewardship. However, one thing is blatantly missing in this judgment: the Creator does not fire them. At no point are they excused from their created duty of stewardship. This, then, is the root of our ongoing struggle with stewardship. From Adam to each of us, the vocation of steward, which was created to be exercised in a perfect garden in the full view of the gracious Creator-Owner, is now carried out by failed and fallen stewards in a broken world that seeks to break us.

These consequences are still with us today. While the vocation of steward is ours by virtue of our creation, we daily fail through idolatry. Idolatry means death, both now and forever. False gods devour their devotees. Humans who seek their lives in food and drink, in work and play, in religion or irreligion, are consumed by the gods they make. We lose, but never find, our lives.[11] Our hands continue to turn over, reach out, and take what is not ours. We still claim ownership of a creation that is not ours. We think of life and life's resources as things to be claimed, counted, and closely held as an attempt to cover up for our naked, albeit failed, claim on divinity. The quest for wealth, possessions, status, and acclaim is what leads many of us to an early grave. We work ourselves to death in the vain attempt to own that which only belongs to God. Marriages fail. Children are a hindrance rather than a blessing. Creation is used, abused, and tossed aside like a used hamburger wrapper, all under our false claim of ownership. When stewards fail by attempting to become owners, both creation and the stewards suffer. There is no glory for creation or its stewards and only grief for the Creator.

STEWARDSHIP SOLUTION

The stewardship crisis of Genesis 3 leaves Creator, stewards, and creation in a terrible mess, a mess that needs to be fixed. But the failed stewards and the broken creation are powerless to save themselves. The cheap sweater that creation has become at the hands of the idolatrous stewards will continue to unravel and expose the shameful nakedness of generations of stewards. The Creator cannot simply excuse the failed stewards. The stewards cannot earn restoration to their rightful vocation. The creation continues to lose. A solution is desperately needed.

The solution is proposed within the crisis. As the Creator pronounces his judgment on the serpent, he includes a promise: "I will put enmity between you and the woman, and between your offspring and her offspring; he shall bruise your head, and you shall bruise his heel" (Gen 3:15). The God who had spoken creation into existence promises to enter creation itself. This would be no pleasure trip. He would become the seed of salvation. He would come to steward the will of

God to its fullness in a way that the first stewards were unable to do. In the process, this seed will crush the head of the serpent while enduring the serpent's fangs in his heel. In the fullness of time, this promised seed came. Jesus was born of woman, born under the law, to redeem those under the curse of the law. Jesus perfectly stewarded the will of God. In him we see who the Father really is. He is no vengeful owner seeking redress for the first stewards' theft. In the life, death, and resurrection of Jesus, we see the perfect stewardship that is the gospel. The cross of Calvary is where the debt is paid. The empty tomb of Easter is the receipt. Paid in full by the sinless Son of God, our debt is satisfied. The idolatrous stewards are redeemed.

As we stewards were not created as ends in ourselves, we are also not redeemed to be ends in ourselves. Once tasked with stewarding the entire creation, now redeemed stewards are functionally tasked with stewarding the one thing we need most: the gospel of Jesus Christ. St. Paul captures this by telling the Corinthians,

> Therefore, if anyone is in Christ, he is a new creation. The old has passed away; behold, the new has come. All this is from

God, who through Christ reconciled us to himself and gave us the ministry of reconciliation; that is, in Christ God was reconciling the world to himself, not counting their trespasses against them, and entrusting to us the message of reconciliation. Therefore, we are ambassadors for Christ, God making his appeal through us. (2 Cor 5:17–20)

This great gift of the gospel is what then restores the *why* of Christian stewardship. We have been created to bear the image of God as stewards. Now, in the new creation of Christ's redeeming work, we are remade in that image. As stewards, we bear the image of Christ in the act of reconciliation that we receive. We steward this by being reconciled with those around us as well. In this ministry of reconciliation, we are stewards of what God has made for the sake of the gospel.

This is a fundamental difference between the way a Christian sees stewardship and the way the world sees it. Some in the world who use the word "stewardship," for example, seek to steward the environment. They have a quest to provide clean air, clear water, and pure soil. On the *how* and *what* levels, the faithful Christian would concur with them. On the *why* level, however, there is a great deal of difference. Non-Christian environmental stewards carry out their stewardship in fear. If the air, water, and soil are not clean, we will all die! Christian stewards come from a vastly different perspective. They see the environment as something to be stewarded because the Lord has created it by speaking, redeemed it in the work of Jesus, and used it as a tool for reconciliation with one's neighbor. This stewardship flows from God's grace through faith in Jesus Christ.

If any chapter in all the Scriptures highlights this new perspective, it is Romans 12. This chapter, penned by St. Paul, serves as a primer for the life of redeemed stewards. Paul writes:

> I appeal to you therefore, brothers, by the mercies of God, to present your bodies as a living sacrifice, holy and acceptable to God, which is your spiritual worship. Do not be conformed to this world, but be transformed by the renewal of your mind, that by testing you may discern what is the will of God, what is good and acceptable and perfect. (Rom 12:1–2)

Paul equates the stewardship life with the sanctified life. They are one and the same because they have the same source. The gospel is God's work. What Jesus accomplished on the cross is not of our own doing. It is this mercy that begets the faithful stewardship of offering our bodies as living sacrifices. Holiness and acceptable worship are beyond us apart from God's work in our life. By extension, both salvation and stewardship are free gifts to us from God.

The Apostles' Creed helps us see this. As we confess the ancient faith in its articles, we encounter creation, redemption, and sanctification: the Father creates; the Son redeems; the Holy Spirit sanctifies, that is, makes us holy. While it is confessed in the classical order, it applies to us in the reverse. The Holy Spirit creates faith in us. This faith connects us to the work of Jesus, who then shows us the true heart of the Father. Again, this is God's gift. In the same way, stewardship is our response to the new relationship we have with the Father through Jesus' work, using the created gifts he gives us.

Stewardship Is Pastoral Care

Since stewardship is God at work in us, it is not simply a matter of program and policy; it is theology. In the seminary setting, stewardship is firmly placed in the school of practical theology. Teaching stewardship is often a challenge because the seminary is a place of theory. It is hard to do practical theology in a theoretic setting. As a result, it is often left to be included as a component of a larger discussion of pastoral theology. But this creates a serious problem once the pastors these seminaries graduate enter the congregational setting.

When a congregation is confronted with the need to support a ministry that gets more expensive every year, the lines connecting stewardship to practical theology are blurred, morphing stewardship into a matter of "pragmatic" theology in the worst sense of the word. This pragmatic theology is no longer worried about the truth of the stewardship *why* but focuses completely on the stewardship *what* and *how*. The standard is no longer "Is it true?" but "Does it work?" And by "work," it means "pay the bills."

A pragmatic theology of stewardship is not stewardship at all. It is severed from its roots in the gospel and creation. When stewardship is severed from the word of God, it withers. This withering is exacerbated when it is grafted onto the weed called "paying the bills." It ceases to be free and joyous.

It becomes a necessary evil that is nothing more than the cost of doing the business of ministry. It is driven by the law and is thus open to manipulation, which leaves the steward a prisoner of guilt. This is not the stewardship for which God has created us!

Stewardship is not a program. Programs deal with *how* and *what*. That kind of approach does not allow for seeking to connect the stewards entrusted to our pastoral care with their identity in creation and redemption. Faithful steward leaders who seek to care pastorally for the sheep entrusted to them will first remind them who they are before prompting them to act. At times, this work will be marked by a call to repentance and the pronouncement of God's rich forgiveness that is theirs in Jesus Christ. This kind of faithful pastoral care will illustrate that what is important to God is not their activity but their identity. Then, the free exercise of stewardship can flow from God through the steward to others. The center of this is the gospel.

The journey of this pastoral care must begin in the right place. For it to reach the destination of a steward freely and joyously carrying out God's will in the gospel of Jesus Christ for the sake of their neighbor and the glory of God, it must start with *why*.

Why are we stewards? God made us this way.

Why are we stewards? Jesus died to restore us to life in this reflection of God's image.

Why are we stewards? We have received the gospel to share it by the way we care for the treasures entrusted to us by God.

The stewardship-as-pastoral-care journey has been laid out. It starts with *why*.

The Teaching and Preaching of Stewardship

Heath R. Curtis

STEWARDSHIP IS PASTORAL CARE, AND THE task of pastoral care is theological in nature. It's not enough that a stewardship program works. A lot of things might work, especially if your definition of "work" is that more money comes into the offering plate. But if you want lasting change in your congregation, change that builds up the people of God into more faithful Christians, then you need to care enough about your members to teach them the *why* of Christian stewardship. And so, you need to evaluate your current teaching and *how* that teaching happens, then determine with planning and purpose how it might change for the better.

In those first dark days of my congregation's financial crisis, I was simply at a loss for where to begin. Things certainly had to change. More money was going out than coming in. The bank had canceled the line of credit. Things had to change ... but what? Should I attack the problem from the direction of spending—get with the school board and trustees and look for places to cut? Or on the income side, should we look to third-source funding for the school, bigger fund raisers, a special plea sent out to every household? A quick rundown of the numbers showed we were about 40 percent short of what we needed for ministry. How do you cut 40 percent of your ministry costs? How can you increase income by 40 percent?

I saw a financial problem and started to think in terms of a financial answer. Math questions call for math answers. And this didn't look good.

But you see what's missing here: theology, the word of God, and the care of souls. The shock of the financial problem and my desire for a quick fix were steering me away from my vocation as a pastor. I'm not a financial adviser. My calling isn't to create the budget, trim costs, or increase revenue. I needed a wakeup call: "Damn it, Jim, you're a pastor, not a CEO!" I needed to act like a pastor, that is, a shepherd. I needed to pray to the Good Shepherd for guidance to tend the flock he had set me over. And I needed to do my job and not try to be something I wasn't.

I was not powerless, but I was also not in control. I didn't have to sit by and watch this train wreck with nothing to do; I had a lot of work that would keep me plenty busy. But I could not control the outcome of that work; that was in the Lord's hands. I was called to do my job faithfully and trust in the Lord to bring it to fruition.

To focus myself, I reread my ordination vows. One of them was this: "Admonish and encourage the people to confidence in Christ and godly living." Teach them, encourage them, *care for their souls.* If that ended up balancing the budget, fine and dandy. But first things first: I needed to be faithful to the vows I made to the Lord. I needed to care for the people as beloved lambs of the Good Shepherd.

This financial crisis was not the ultimate crisis; it was a symptom. The issue was theological and pastoral, and the solution was "confidence in Christ and godly living." And teaching that certainly was my job.

Teaching in Your Congregation

If you knew that 50 percent of the members of your congregation were committing adultery, would you spend a little extra time on that commandment? If 40 percent of your members were embezzling funds from work, a little extra emphasis on "Thou shalt not steal" would probably be in order.

I can almost guarantee you that far fewer than half of the members of your congregation are giving a faithful, generous, sacrificial, firstfruits proportion of their income (1 Cor 16) toward the ministry of your church. Check the data—from sources like the Pew Research Center, the Barna Group, or your own denomination—and that truth will be confirmed.[12] This kind of giving doesn't just happen. It takes teaching and encouragement. Of course, this is why Jesus and St. Paul teach and encourage it in the New Testament, and why it's touched on by both Moses and Malachi in the Old Testament.

In the last chapter, we laid out some fresh theological perspectives on the vocation of steward to get your theological gears in motion and help you appreciate aspects of the biblical message you may not have noticed before. If your gears are now in motion, you've probably already made some more notes with your own insights. That's the *what* of teaching stewardship, which chapter 4 will cover. But now it's time to talk about the *how*. How does this teaching happen in your congregation? Before you can make it better, you have to understand what is happening now and consider it from both the pastor's perspective and the layperson's. To help you think about this, let's walk through the ways and places in which teaching happens. I'll save the pulpit, the most important place, for last because your plan for preaching will be greatly enhanced if you first consider all the other teaching contexts.

PLACES, PEOPLE, AND TEACHING

Changing the stewardship culture of a congregation is a huge task. It takes a lot of patient teaching. Coordinating that teaching across all these places and people is a must. This requires both an intentional plan for preaching and a commitment to track the participation and response of those being led in stewardship.

Where does teaching happen in your congregation? Certainly, the pulpit. But it also happens in classrooms, such as in Sunday school classes and Bible studies. Perhaps your congregation also has formal teaching off campus, like small group studies in member homes. And what about meeting rooms? Do the various board and committee meetings start with devotions that could be used as teaching?

What is the current level of coordination among all these places? Does the Sunday school lesson follow the topic of the Sunday worship service? Do all the small groups study the same topic at the same time? Is there any coordinated plan for the devotions at board meetings?

Who's doing the teaching in your congregation? Certainly, the pastor is. But also Sunday school teachers, small group leaders, committee chairs, and, most importantly of all, parents.[13]

If you are going to teach your entire congregation a new way of thinking about generosity and the vocation of steward, you're going to need all your teachers on the same page. That's one thing when you're talking about paid church staff and quite another when you're talking about volunteers and parents. Here are some diagnostic questions:

- What's your congregational culture of gathering and training teachers? Are so many wanting to teach that you're turning people away? Or are you always begging for warm bodies to serve as Sunday school teachers?

- Do you think of parents as teachers? How can they be engaged?

- Are any age groups in your congregation underrepresented in the teaching role? Who could you recruit to teach in those underrepresented groups?

- Why don't people volunteer to teach? Identify the barriers by actually asking the folks who turn you down.

- How long are you asking people to commit to teaching? A key barrier for younger generations is the time commitment. If you ask for a shorter time commitment, say six weeks instead of a whole school year, you may find that you'll have more than enough volunteers for Sunday school and Bible classes.

Who's being taught in your congregation? Every church treats members as students; everyone is invited to come to a Sunday school class or a Bible study. But many churches fail to treat their leaders as students. A congregation-wide push to learn about biblical generosity requires an engaged and willing lay leadership. This is especially true if, like about two-thirds of the congregations in my own denomination, your church has not done much intentional teaching on stewardship for some time.

Think about your congregation as a group of concentric circles. The largest circle is your entire worshiping membership.[14] In the center circle are the pastor and professional staff. This group, of course, has to be on the same page for anything productive to get done in the church's life. If there is conflict here, you'll need to reconcile before you can take any meaningful steps toward addressing stewardship in the congregation.

But what circles exist between the pastor(s) and the whole worshiping congregation? In my own parish, it goes like this: pastor, elders, church council, all the church officers, worshiping congregation. Your church may have a different structure. And beyond this, your actual structure might be different from whatever is written down in your church constitution or bylaws. You need to make your own concentric-circle leadership map of your congregation. Who are the people who absolutely must be on board for this stewardship teaching push to work? In my own parish, if the pastor and elders are united on something, it's gonna get done. If we aren't on the same page, it stops right there and we pause, teach, learn, and pray until we are on the same page.

Plan on beginning your stewardship teaching with the center of the concentric circles and then working your way out. Teach the word with confidence in those smaller, inner circles, and then, as you move to the larger circles, you will have a stronger base of support. You may even want to divide that largest circle (the worshiping community) into smaller groups. I found this to be vital to the initial stewardship effort in my parish. Your parish may do much better, but in my church, only about 30 percent of the adults attend my Sunday Bible class. This teaching about stewardship calls for a level of interaction that only a smaller group can afford. So in my overall plan for teaching, I decided to institute a "Brunch with Pastor" phase in which my wife and I would host eight to ten members at a time, share a meal, and recap the stewardship teaching they had been hearing on Sunday morning.

Take a layered approach. You cannot ever communicate or teach too much. The congregation is now made up of more generations than ever before. You cannot assume that your elderly are not online. Neither can you be confident that your younger members will be willing or able to find your communication in the wash of electronic media that inundates them daily. Overseeding is key.

Ask yourself: Where do your people get their teaching? And how much of it can you influence? Is your congregation social media savvy? Does your denomination produce a lot of radio and podcast resources? Do your people use daily devotion books?

Note that you *control* only some of these technologies in whole or in part. You might have a podcast, but your people might listen to a dozen others. You produce a monthly newsletter and a weekly bulletin, but your people use something else every day. Obviously, you need to plan for the content you will use in the resources you control (for example, your social media posts, your sermons, your online devotions). But give serious thought to other resources that you can *recommend*. What podcasts or radio shows do you want your people listening to? Is there a book on a given topic or a daily devotional book you wish your board of elders were reading? Don't be shy about making pastoral recommendations and leveraging all of these different technologies to reach your goals in teaching your people.

Time and Teaching

You've probably already noticed that this is going to take a long time. Exactly how long should this take? And what if my congregation is in crisis right now?

Back in 2006, my congregation was in a right-now crisis. But we did not have a right-now answer. If we were going to get into a stable position, the people had to be taught the word. For that teaching to be effective, the whole congregation had to come along together. For that to work, I knew I would have to get the elders on board, then the church council, then all the officers. I would have to teach this thoroughly in Bible class and allow people to digest it, ask questions, and pick it apart. I would be leading meetings with devotions based on this; I'd be talking to the Sunday school teachers; I'd have to find a way to engage the entire congregation in smaller groups (those brunches with pastor). All of this was going to take time.

So if you are in crisis right now, you'll have to find a way to muddle through while you actually fix the problems. It's a bit like learning that you have a cracked foundation, or that an expensive repair is needed on your car, and you just don't have the cash right now. You have to find a way to get by until the full fix can be handled properly. You might be riding the bus for a while or caulking that crack until you can get the foundation mud-jacked into proper position. There is no shortcut to the proper fix.

So how long will this take? You should plan on at least nine months, and a whole year is better. You've got to *teach* the people what the word of God says; you've got to *ask* them whether they are going to do it; and then you must *plan accordingly*. If you do that, things will be better than if you don't. But clearly, it takes careful planning, faithful execution, and time.

The payoff is worth it. I'm not telling you that if you follow this process, you will never have any more problems or your offering plate giving will go up and up forever. But if you take your time and do it right, your people will respond to the word of God, change their behavior, and move in the right direction. Challenges and crises will arise, but these will be easier to face if you take the time to fashion a proper stewardship culture and a balanced budget based on the people's informed generosity.

That's what I found when the time came for my congregation to face our next crisis. We came through that first year of focused, planned, intentional, across-the-board stewardship teaching, and by 2007, we had our first balanced budget in who-knows-how-many years. The people listened to the word. They changed their habits. They pledged to give in a newly generous way, and then they outgave their pledges. (I suspect that this last fact had more to do with being conservative Midwesterners than anything else: under-promise and over-perform!)

The school was saved. The budget was balanced. The temperature on every conflict seemed to be turned down. So life in our congregation was good.

And then came 2012. The giving did not rise to the level of what was pledged. The 2008 financial crisis had taken a while to hit our community on the edge of the cornfield and the St. Louis metro area. But when it hit, it came with a double whammy. First, the steel mill where several of my members worked shut its doors. While that was rippling through the industrial economy of our area, a terrible drought shocked the agricultural sector. Financial Crisis 2.0 was upon us.

But we had developed a new culture, a culture of taking the time to teach the word, ask the people to respond, and plan the budget accordingly. And so the elders and I could make a plan for how to face this crisis. We laid out a plan to do something different with Christian education that would lead us to pull out of the parish school partnership while still providing tuition assistance for our students to attend Christian school elsewhere. We put the plan together and hoped that in 2013 we would see things turn around; if not, we'd put the plan into motion. Then, things only got more difficult in the local economy. It was time to execute the plan. It was hard. The tradeoff was painful: our member children would still get a Christian education, but our own campus would not have active classrooms with laughing children, and jobs would be lost. It was hard, but it was responsible and doable, and everyone embraced the plan and moved forward.

Because we had taken the time to do this right, we knew what our actual financial capacity was. We had established a long track record of living within our means. Our future path was clear, even if it included some pain. I lost a lot of sleep and two inches on my waist as this plan came together. But on the other side, we are a stronger congregation, and in 2016, our giving had recovered enough that we were able to catch up on a lot of deferred maintenance on our property.

Take the time to plan this out and do it right; it's worth it.

Preaching in Your Congregation

This is what the church cannot do without: preaching. Jesus traveled around preaching. He sent out the seventy-two to preach to all the cities in Israel that the kingdom of God was at hand. Peter preached to the crowds on Pentecost. In Acts 20, Paul preached until midnight to the people gathered on the Lord's Day (much to the chagrin of Eutychus). The apostles went to all nations preaching the good news. Paul summarizes his ministry this way: "We preach Christ crucified" (1 Cor 1:23). The preaching office is necessary for the church and her mission: "How then will they call on him in whom they have not believed? And how are they to believe in him of whom they have never heard? And how are they to hear without someone preaching?" (Rom 10:14).

The pastor's preaching is the hub of the congregation's teaching ministry. Everything comes together here. The who: everyone is gathered to hear the pastor's preaching, including every age, every activity level, and every level of service; all the others who share in some aspect of teaching are now hearing and learning from the chief teacher. The where: everyone is gathered in from all the other places where your church's ministry happens; now there is just one place with one voice leading. You can record the sermon, broadcast it live online or on the radio, or distribute it as the written word, but every technology proves its ultimate usefulness only insofar as it can help us multiply the reach of the preaching event. The life of the church cannot do without this. This is what the church boils down to: the people gathered together as the body of Christ to hear the called minister preach Christ's word.

So if you are going to move the congregation into a new way of thinking and acting regarding stewardship, you need to evaluate and plan your preaching for this nine-to-twelve-month period of intentional teaching on the biblical doctrine of stewardship. You have a lot to do during this time. Think back to all those concentric circles of people who need to be taught. Think of the Bible studies you'll want to put together, the meetings you'll need to lead with your other teachers and leaders. Your preaching throughout this period needs to support and lead all of that.

It's not that you'll be preaching on stewardship for thirty-six weeks straight. And don't just slip in a stewardship line in every sermon. A four-week series at either the beginning or the end of this time period isn't the way to go, either. Instead, this grand project of changing the church's entire viewpoint and action on a specific topic is a great opportunity for you to rethink your administration of the preaching office from beginning to end.

Preaching Three Ways

If you are part of a church with a strong liturgical tradition, then you are used to thinking about your preaching in terms of a yearly cycle. But the truth is that every church does this to one extent or another; we all celebrate Christmas in December and Easter in the spring. We all follow a basic yearly cycle focusing on the life, death, and resurrection of Jesus Christ. But how we preach through the year differs. Generally speaking, there are three approaches: a lectionary, sermon series, and *lectio continua*.

Most churches primarily use one of these methods, although almost every congregation uses aspects of each at different times.

Which method is best for tackling this journey of teaching your congregation about stewardship? I might as well ask if it's better to preach from notes, a full manuscript, or an outline; to use slides, notes in the bulletin, or no visual aids all. You have to be you. Each of these methods can be effective within its own context as long as you take the time for careful planning.

Each method does have its own pros and cons when it comes to preaching and teaching on stewardship. As you think through your own plans, make this teaching natural and organic to your way of preaching; it should not feel artificial or tacked on.

A lectionary. The Sunday morning Scripture readings are predetermined by an authority that exists above and outside of the local congregation, and the preaching follows these predetermined texts. A lectionary may make its way through the Bible over the course of one year or three. My own way of preaching in a liturgical church is via a lectionary, so when I was making my plans for preaching stewardship over the course of a year,

I sat down with the lectionary and went through every week of the year. Which Sundays had texts that lent themselves to this topic? Where did they fall in the year? How many were there? How did that map onto my plan for reaching the concentric circles of the congregation with this teaching? An advantage to preaching stewardship with a lectionary is that everything will come across as very natural: these are just the readings for the given Sunday; I'm not tacking anything on in an artificial way. The challenge is that the time is not up to you. The lectionary may indeed drive the timing of your path through the concentric circles of your congregation.

Sermon series. Within American evangelicalism, this is probably the most popular model of preaching through the year. The pastor (or the pastoral staff in larger congregations) determines a biblical topic to explore and lays out a Scripture reading plan for a course of weeks. The length of each series will vary. There might be one or two readings each Sunday that focus on the topic.

The challenges and opportunities are different in this case. On the one hand, you have a lot more control over where to put these topics in the course of the year. You can choose which topics come before or after a stewardship series. The length is up to you; you may run a six-week series or two different three-week series. But just like the pastor who is using a lectionary, a big part of your planning needs to be mapping your preaching against your plan to reach the concentric circles of your congregation.

Lectio continua. This is preaching through an entire book of the Bible. In the early centuries of the church's life, this was a very popular method of preaching during the week. On Sunday, the lectionary focused on walking through the life of Jesus in a yearly cycle, but at the weekday services, which every congregation seemed to hold, the preacher would simply read a few verses of a book each day and preach on them until he had preached through the entire book. For example, today we have sermons on the entire book of Matthew from St. John Chrysostom because he preached through that book during the weekday services in Constantinople. (It took him ninety sermons!)

For churches that make regular use of *lectio continua*, timing may be the chief challenge. If you are currently on Jeremiah 5, you might have to detour out of that prophet for a while to insert some New

Testament books that deal with stewardship in a more direct way. Again, whichever books you decide to preach, you need to map that preaching plan over your plan for teaching through the concentric circles of your leadership.

Don't be afraid to borrow a page from one of the other preaching methods. Even if you are from a lectionary church, like me, you will find special observances as options in your lectionary. So, for example, I use the Harvest Festival readings for our commitment Sunday. In fact, I run a bit of a series in the fall with three lectionary-approved special observances (Christian Education, Mission Festival, and Harvest Festival) replacing part of the Trinity Season (the time between Pentecost and Advent).

Likewise, if you regularly use sermon series, here are two lessons you can take from the world of the lectionary. First, the lectionary tends to spread teachings on a topic throughout the year. I would advise you to use several shorter series on different aspects of stewardship throughout this nine-to-twelve-month period rather than trying to do it all in a single four- or six-week series. This will allow time for the seeds of teaching and preaching to germinate and take root in your hearers. Second, the lectionary does a great job of combining biblical texts. For example, here are the readings assigned for the Fifteenth Sunday after Trinity in the one-year lectionary: Psalm 86; 1 Kings 17:8–16 (the widow at Zarephath); Galatians 5:25–6:10; and Matthew 6:24–34. Take those apart, and you've got a four-week stewardship series right there!

And who can argue with the wisdom of *lectio continua*? Reading through a book of the Bible, perhaps especially an epistle that was originally read in church in its entirety as a letter, is simply a good practice. The Revised Common Lectionary added a lot more of this style into its Epistle readings in the long season of time between Pentecost and Advent. Pastor Meador and I even call our stewardship workshop for pastors and lay leaders *The Philippians Workshop* because reading through that book from start to finish will give you keen insights into how faithful stewardship affects the church's life.

No matter which method or combination of methods you choose, my overall point is this: *you have to make a plan for this preaching.* You need to be intentional. And you need to think about your preaching as leading the teaching journey through the concentric circles of your church's structure.

Preaching Content and Form

We have addressed the *how* of preaching and teaching stewardship as it flows out of the *what* of stewardship. Now, a final thought about the manner in which the *how* of our preaching changes based on *what* we are teaching.

After the resurrection, Jesus summed up the content of Christian preaching this way:

> Thus it is written, that the Christ should suffer and on the third day rise from the dead, and that repentance for the forgiveness of sins should be proclaimed in his name to all nations, beginning from Jerusalem. (Luke 24:46–47)

> Go into all the world and proclaim the gospel to the whole creation. (Mark 16:15)

We proclaim the gospel, the good news, that we have forgiveness of sins in and through Christ when we repent of our sins and cling to him alone in faith. Every other doctrine that we preach must be connected to and support this central teaching.

Some teachings are easy to connect to the gospel: the doctrine of the person of Christ; the doctrine of baptism; the doctrine of the return of Christ. It's even easy to connect the

Ten Commandments: you haven't kept them, and therefore, you need a Savior! That basic format of sin and grace, law and gospel, commands and promises, is right there in Peter's first sermon in Acts 2 and runs like a golden thread through all of the New Testament epistles.

But how does stewardship fit into this weekly preaching structure? How can we instruct people in the law without becoming legalists? In chapter 2, we showed you a theological way of tackling this problem. But now we need to think about how to do this homiletically; we need to translate that theological content into a homiletical technique.

Preaching styles vary, and there are a thousand different plans for how to write a sermon that conveys the basic message of the New Testament. We don't need to review all of the styles and plans that are appropriate. But in one way or another, I think the week-in, week-out preaching of a gospel-focused pastor should have as its basis, its super-structure, if you will, this proclamation of sin and grace. The natural movement of this sort of proc-lamatory sermon is seen not only in Peter's sermon from Acts 2 but also in Nathan's confrontation of David in 2 Samuel 12. It goes from confronting the hearers with their sins in the face of God's law, to calling them to a life of repentance, to comforting them with the sacrifice of Christ, to assuring them that they can receive this comfort in Christ today along with the strength to lead a godly Christian life by his word and Spirit.

That's an outline of Christian preaching that is displayed throughout the Bible. If you look through some of your old sermons, you'll likely see that general flow again and again, even if you were not thinking about it when you were writing the sermon. It's just a biblical pattern of thinking and speaking that we have picked up by osmosis.

It's helpful to think about adding specific instruction on a specific teaching to this basic biblical model. When I want to add instruction to a sermon, it is usually slotted in after the third or fourth movements. I will then circle back with a repetition of that movement.

So, for example, a Christmas sermon might run like this.

I.   The angels come to see the shepherds— not the religious leaders, not the priests, not the Pharisees. Why? Because, as we'll see in the rest of the New Testament, the Pharisees don't want to hear the good news of Jesus because they don't think they need him. They think they are doing fine, doing their best. I wonder: In what ways do we think we are sufficient without Jesus? In what ways do we think our best is good enough?

II. This calls for self-examination and repentance.

III. But I've got good news, the same good news the angels brought to the shepherds: in spite of Pharisees old and new, the Christ has come to Bethlehem that he might march to Calvary, where he shed his blood for you.

IV. You are washed white indeed in the water of baptism. The Lord has cleansed you and given you a new life. It's time to live for him.

Now, let's say I wanted to add a bit of instruction on the person of Christ, or on the Christian versus the Muslim conception of God, or on protecting vulnerable life, all of which fit nicely with the theme and readings for this day. I would probably put that between points III and IV and then circle back to repeat some of III before heading on to IV.

Of course, you can imagine times when the instruction is best placed at the very beginning of the sermon; as I said, a variety of appropriate preaching plans exist. And some sermons will focus almost exclusively on teaching a given topic in theology or practical Christian living. But even preaching based on this biblical pattern of sin and grace, law and gospel, command and promise, has a natural place for teaching stewardship or any other topic in Christian living.

My preaching has changed as I have served the same parish through a decade and a half. I still preach sin and grace. I still preach the same biblical doctrine I swore to preach at my ordination. I still often use the biblical pattern of preaching we've been examining. But I find that as I have grown older and more comfortable in my own skin, my preaching looks more and more like the outline of the book of Romans, not only in order but also in weight of words. After introducing his theme, Paul spends about two and a half chapters on sin and mankind's need for a Savior (chapters 1–3), after which he explains the gospel in great detail and preaches it with power (chapters 3–5). Then for the rest of the book, he turns to the question of Christian living after the gospel has been received. Chapters 6–8 are a riff on the question, "Shall we go on sinning that grace may abound?" Chapters 9–11 deal with a doctrinal topic that arises out of this discussion (election). And then it's back to encouragement, admonishment, and practical instruction for being "a living sacrifice" (chapters 12–16).

I don't think the relative numbers of words Paul spends on each of these topics is random or accidental. Teaching the gospel takes relatively few words. It is a simple message, after all. But encouraging the people to stay in that gospel, admonishing them away from temptation, instructing them in the path of life and in the whole counsel of God— that takes a lot more planning and a lot more words. Keep that thought in mind as you plan your preaching on the vital topic of stewardship.

Conclusion

Changing the stewardship culture in a congregation is a big job. It must be based on and flow from the biblical message, and it must be approached with patience and wisdom. The pastor, as the holder of the preaching office who must care for the souls of the people, will need to spend significant time in preparing this sea change in the church's life. Preaching is where all this comes together. It is how the congregation will learn to align its practice with sound theology. Therefore, the congregation's life flows from the teaching that comes from the pulpit. However, the pastor is not the only teacher. Every aspect of the church's teaching ministry must be aligned. The entire congregation needs to hear this teaching, but the congregation itself is comprised of concentric circles of leadership and involvement. Time must be spent on each circle, from the most central leaders out to the whole worshiping community.

All of this will take careful, intentional planning on the pastor's part, which will take time. But this investment of time and effort will be blessed. The people of God will respond to his word. Your church will move forward in strength.

CHAPTER 4

The Culture of Stewardship

Nathan Meador

We've been working our way through the golden circle of stewardship: the why, the how, and the what. Chapter 2 dealt with the *why* of stewardship: humanity has been created in the image of God, entrusted with his perfect creation, redeemed by Jesus from the sin of our failed stewardship, and restored and equipped for that stewardship by the Holy Spirit. In chapter 3, we dealt with the *how* of stewardship: preaching and teaching stewardship needs to be intentional and consistent, because while the steward is fully redeemed by the blood of Christ, the sinful nature within us still seeks to knock God off his divine throne and claim the glory for ourselves. This nature goes against what we desire. This makes faithful stewardship countercultural, not only in our world but also within each individual steward. The *what* of stewardship is the next step in the development of our story of stewardship. Tackling this *what* requires a discussion of culture.

Culture as Present Reality

Defining the term "culture" is like nailing Jello to the wall. Some define it as the boogeyman of all things orthodox. Pro-life supporters talk about the "culture of death." Those who decry the moral decay in society castigate the "culture of promiscuity." The Me-Too Movement speaks of the "culture of sexual abuse" in the workplace, church, and politics. The boogeyman view of culture is created by our culture of "us versus them" (see, I did it myself!) that has spilled from our political discourse into almost every aspect of life. In this way, the word "culture" almost always carries a negative connotation.

This is an unfortunate development. Culture is not inherently evil. While this may seem a bit simplistic, culture is really nothing more than the way things get done.[15] There is culture everywhere, including in the church. Every congregation has a culture. This includes its customs and underlying attitudes. A church's culture is present in the way the congregation worships, the way it forms the faith in the next generation, the way it governs itself, and even how it has fellowship together. This is true of every congregation that I have served. Your congregation's culture will have its own distinct characteristics as well.

Culture develops in one of two ways. Either a culture is intentionally planned, or it grows organically. Most congregations will have many elements of their culture develop organically. The way things happen becomes the way things are supposed to happen. An apocryphal story illustrates this. A small congregation had a very dedicated church secretary. For her, the greatest sin was a typo in the weekly church bulletin. She prided herself in the pursuit of perfection. One week, there were several major events that needed her attention. She did not get to print the weekend worship bulletin until late Friday afternoon. In her haste, she accidentally ran the bulletin upside down on the pre-purchased bulletin stock. There was no way she could rectify the situation. Exasperated, she called the pastor to confess her clerical sin. The pastor, attempting to make light of the situation, assured her, "After all, it is the Thirteenth Sunday after Pentecost. That is the week the church always prints the bulletin upside down!" A year later, with the pastor now serving a different congregation, he received a call from his former secretary. She asked him, "Now which Sunday is it that we are supposed to print the bulletin upside down?"

This lame attempt at clergy humor is not too far from the way that culture is formed in a congregation. The way things get done often defaults to the experience of the current generation of leadership: "It's how we've always done it." For every example of the way a pastor and leadership have attempted to change the culture of a congregation, there are hundreds of examples in which culture just happens. A mistake, a crisis, or a one-time idea is repeated a few times and becomes the way the congregation has always done it. This can be positive and can support the work of the gospel. But often, these organically developed congregational cultures can negatively impact the kingdom work of the congregation. Culture will never be neutral. It will either enhance gospel ministry or hinder it. Just as an unseen current will cause an un-anchored boat to drift even on a calm day, the culture in a congregation will move either toward faithfulness or away from it.[16] It will never stay stagnant.

This view of congregational culture applies to stewardship as well. Every congregation has a stewardship culture. It, too, has developed by either design or happenstance. A stewardship culture is a set of beliefs and values regarding the relationship of individuals and institutions to money and possessions.[17] (The two stewardship stories in chapter 1 are examples of the stewardship cultures that were created in our congregations and in our lives.) Unfortunately, the dominant stewardship culture in the American church focuses on the survival of the institution and the needs of the congregation. This has become true for more and more congregations because of the skyrocketing cost of doing faithful ministry. In many cases, salary and benefit costs for clergy, the rising costs of insurance for ministry facilities, and staff sizes from previous generations have placed great strain on congregational budgets, which has opened the door to a culture of scarcity. A stewardship culture formed by scarcity will render innovation in ministry impossible and will make even survival a challenge. This kind of culture has lasting impact on the work of the gospel. This culture of scarcity left unchecked can lead to a congregational implosion.

A culture of scarcity finds its roots within the hearts of the sinful stewards in the congregation. In his book *Transforming Stewardship*, C. K. Robertson shares a story that gets at the heart of the congregational stewardship culture challenge:

> There was a story of a group of Viking warriors who were ordered by their king to join him when he converted to the Christian faith through the waters of baptism. As they waded out into the nearby river to be baptized, they all went under the water while holding one of their arms high above their heads. If they had been asked why they were doing this, the warriors would have answered that they did not want the arm and hand that bore the sword to go under the water, for they had been taught that whatever goes under the water belongs to God. These warriors were willing to let the rest of their bodies and, thus, their lives belong to God, but their sword arms would be held back.[18]

When there is a stewardship culture of scarcity, stewards hold back. This is where the identification of a congregation's stewardship culture becomes a matter of pastoral care. Remember, as we mentioned in chapter 2, faltering stewardship is not simply a matter of miserliness or stinginess. It is a matter of idolatry! This idolatry runs rampant in the church. In fact, I often wonder, if baptismal conversion happened today in the same fashion as to the Viking swordsmen of Robertson's example, how many people would go under the water with their wallet, checkbook, or smartphone sticking high in the air, not to protect it from getting wet but because they are unwilling to share those very elements granted to them by God's generosity?

Culture Is Not Set in Stone

While it is true that culture is everywhere, and that it is never neutral in relationship to the work of the gospel, it is also not cast in stone. Organic culture, with its roots in history and practice, can be changed. Culture change is not easy, and it won't happen immediately, but it can be done. It requires intentional planning and great effort.

For example, think of the culture of marriage. Marriage is clearly commanded and defined by

God. The church carried forth this foundational culture for almost 2,000 years. This culture, with some adaptation over the generations, developed organically over a long period of time. Yet, in less than a generation, with intentional effort, the culture of life, same-sex marriage, gender identity, and even the understanding and need for marriage itself has undergone massive change, not only in wider society, but even within the church!

What is true in the culture of life and marriage is also true in the congregational culture of stewardship. It is in no way a matter of the laws of the Medes and Persians. And while change is not easy, it is not only possible but also necessary. When a congregation or individual steward begins to think that they have mastered stewardship, they are missing the point. If a steward has the breath of life, the call to faithful stewardship still applies. Defined by the *why* of stewardship and shaped through the formational *how* of stewardship as found in preaching and teaching, the sanctified life of the stewardship *what* takes place in the daily life of repentance and faith.

While stewardship culture transformation is necessary, the process of change can be daunting. An old axiom in the church states, "It is easier to change doctrine than it is practice." This is a cultural statement. Without a proper grounding in their identity as stewards of the gospel, congregations often confuse who they are with what they do. To start making noise about changing part of the culture—"the way it has always been done"— is a threat to congregational self-concept. The congregational stewardship culture, which has most often developed organically over time, has a strong current. It was not adopted overnight; it will certainly not be changed overnight.

So any attempt at a stewardship culture change needs time. New pastors should move carefully. They should allow a time of thorough observation and interrogation before undertaking any stewardship culture change. This is where pastoral care comes in. It is critical that any cultural change that is undertaken first aligns with Scripture. This change must also be done in a pastorally sensitive way. A bull turned loose in a china shop will reduce the delicate merchandise to shards, and a pastor who plows ahead with a cultural change will have similar effects on his sheep. But by carefully shepherding through teaching and listening and praying and teaching and suggesting and teaching and praying, a pastor can bring about a culture change with little or no collateral damage.

Here is one final point on changing a steward-ship culture: it does not take consensus. If culture change hinges on consensus, it will never happen. There will always be the blessed saint or saints who adopt the "My answer is NO! Do not confuse me with facts" approach, and so waiting on consensus creates a tyranny of the minority. This is neither healthy for the congregation nor godly. The anti-dote to this tyranny is for the pastor and leaders to be committed to a life of biblical stewardship. This commitment is communicated regularly and con-sistently over time. Soon, a tipping point is reached, and the new culture is firmly in place without great resistance (again, the cultural changes in our world illustrate this reality). As little as 20–25 percent of an active congregation can engineer this kind of transformative cultural change.

Celebration and Repentance

The transition to a more faithful stewardship cul-ture begins with celebration. I am not talking about throwing a party. What I am suggesting is really a celebration of thanksgiving—give thanks for what's good in the culture that already exists.

Every congregation has a stewardship culture. The congregations we serve have both been around for over a century and a half. Our personal stewardship stories did not find the stewardship stories of our congregations as blank slates. There are generations of faithful stewards whom the Lord has gathered around these two altars. They have prayed, praised, and petitioned the Lord of the church over this time. Because of this legacy of stewardship, these congregations are still here today. Unless you are serving a totally new church plant made up entirely of first-generation Christian converts, your congregation will have a stewardship culture too. This is a clear testimony that no congregational stewardship culture is completely bad and needs a total overhaul; to think otherwise is the height of either ignorance or arrogance.

Attempting to change a stewardship culture without having an appreciation for the history of the congregation is a recipe for disaster. A pastor who is attempting a stewardship culture change must make every effort to know as much as possible about the defining moments of the congregation. These defining moments are often positive. They may hinge around their founding pastors and leaders. Other positive defining moments can be the building of a new sanctuary, the launch of a new ministry, or a deepening commitment to mission beyond the congregation. A challenge to ministry that was met and overcome, like many congregations are experiencing amid the pandemic during which this book is being written, can also serve as a rallying point for positives in a stewardship culture. Celebrate these positive defining moments as you lead your congregation's stewardship culture change.

As you examine your congregation's stewardship culture and history, you will also uncover negative defining moments that need to be assessed. The sudden death or moral failing of a pastor or key leader can devastate a congregation's culture for the long term. A natural disaster that destroyed the church building or severely hampered ministry, the closure of a long-term ministry like a school or childcare center, or the depopulation of rural areas can also leave negative impacts on a stewardship culture.

A pastoral approach to stewardship will need to evaluate how the congregation understands and practices stewardship. It is important to know if regular worship attenders who are giving of the treasures God has entrusted to them are doing this because the Lord is truly the Owner and they are but stewards, or merely because they want to meet the budget and preserve the institution. Any assessment of a congregational stewardship culture must also seek to determine if the members of the congregation see stewardship as extending beyond financial matters and into their entire lives.

There is also a corporate aspect to assessing a congregation's stewardship culture. The way leaders manage the resources that the Lord entrusts to them for ministry through the congregation's individual stewards can either hinder or help individual stewardship. The ways congregational leaders establish, manage, and report the budget and finances have a great deal of influence on stewardship. Secrecy, dishonesty, and a lack of transparency murder individual stewardship. Careless spending and large operating deficits are not only poor stewardship but also sins against the stewards entrusted to the pastor's care. When stewardship is taught as nothing more than the annual budget drive and not a daily call to repentance and new life for both the congregation and each individual steward, the pastor and leaders of the congregation are stewardship wolves in sheep's clothing.

Stewardship culture change is really a call for the pastoral care of stewards, and it begins with a call to celebration. The faithful history and practice of stewardship in your congregation needs to be celebrated and strengthened. Tell the stories of the faithful stewards in the past. Highlight them as sermon illustrations and in communication pieces. Highlight the faithful practices of past leaders and families who have made the current ministry possible. Hold them up, not for veneration but as examples to follow. After all, that is how humans learn: we watch; we study; we emulate. Taking strengths and making them stronger is the way to faithfully, effectively teach stewardship.

When your assessment of the congregational stewardship culture finds areas that are lacking, it also becomes a call to repentance. When Christians are caught in sin, repentance is the first step. The first step in new life happens when the Lord uses his word to convict of sin and expose the death that comes with it. When sinners steeped in sin come to their senses, like the prodigal in Luke 15, they return home! What greets them is a heavenly Father who has created and redeemed them for this wonderfully fulfilling ministry of stewardship for the sake of the gospel. Forgiveness of sins meets the repenting stewards, and a new life is created. A forgiven steward baptized into Christ is, as St. Paul reminds the Corinthians, a new creation. The old has gone; the new has come (2 Cor 5:17)!

A Story of Stewardship
Transformation

Nowhere in Scripture is there a clearer example of a stewardship culture transformation than the story of Zacchaeus in Luke 19. Zacchaeus is a sinful sell-out, a traitor to his people. What makes him most despicable is that he extorts from his own nation for both the Roman government and his own self-interest. He cares about no one other than himself. That is, until he meets Jesus. Or better yet, until Jesus comes to him, not only to call him out but also to dine with him. This encounter with Jesus produces the change. It does not come from within Zacchaeus. Jesus invites himself in; his presence is what produces the transformation. In the course of one dinner, a selfish thief gives half of what he has to the poor and then promises to double the restitution that the law requires. How does Jesus sum up this encounter? He makes it clear that salvation had come to that house. The lost had been found! But Zacchaeus' giving itself was not the salvific transformation; rather, it was the fruit of the transformation. A redeemed steward is one whose stewardship reflects the image of the one who had created him in the first place and then redeemed him out of his sinfulness.

This stewardship culture change happens the same way in both individuals and the congregations. It is not about a plan or a program. The key to this kind of lasting transformation is a matter of pastoral care. It is about getting sinful stewards to Jesus and letting him do his work through the gospel. Jesus' presence was enough to turn Zacchaeus around. The same presence of our Lord through his word is what will turn stewards around today. Our churches' pews are filled with Zacchaeuses. They are very often looking out for themselves and the enemy rather than the Creator. Remember, failed stewardship is idolatry. Cultivating a culture of stewardship flowing from the gospel is the antidote to that eternally damning idolatry.

Looking to the Harvest

Grandpa Meador was a frustrated farmer who made a living as a truck driver. When the Meadors retired, they moved back to central Illinois. The jet-black soil was a farmer's dream. They had a huge garden that any city kid would call a field. They grew tomatoes and potatoes, sweet corn and sweet peas, cucumbers, and kohlrabi. Grandpa was also especially well known for his home-grown popcorn. There was nothing like helping can and freeze the produce of that garden, especially when we knew that some of it would end up as our Christmas gifts. Opening a pint of that frozen sweet corn in January was like opening a summer day in the middle of winter.

This gardening success did not come without planning or thought. While Grandpa was the farmer, Grandma was the planner. One of Grandma's favorite times of year was when the seed catalog came in the mail. This was when the planning took place. She knew which varieties tasted good and grew the best. She placed the order, and Grandpa tilled the soil. Those midwinter days were signs of hope. Without them and the planning that came with them, there would be no harvest. Nor did that harvest come on the first day of spring. No, it took planning, effort, and time.

When a pastor seeks to bring a congregation's stewardship culture in line with Scripture, he needs to be in touch with his inner Grandma Meador.

It takes planning. The soil needs to be prepared. The right varieties need to be ordered and planted. Weeding needs to be done. There is a long time between seed catalog and harvest. In stewardship culture change, the steps are similar. The culture is assessed. A new culture is envisioned. The new culture is then embodied. Finally, the new culture takes shape. Skip a step or cut corners, and the harvest will be endangered.

First, as we discussed earlier in the chapter, assess the stewardship culture. Ask the following questions: What are the defining moments of this congregation? What does the term "stewardship" mean to the members of the congregation? Do the people give to sustain the budget or in response to God's created call to be stewards of his possessions? Do the members see stewardship as more than just giving? Does it include their entire lives? How does the congregation normally teach stewardship? How does the congregation set its budget?

These questions are not meant to simply be put to the rank-and-file church members in the form of a survey. Surveys have a place in ministry, but not here. They are best addressed in a focus group setting. If you have a neighboring pastor or denominational official who can ask these questions, it can lead to even better answers. (You do not, however, need a high-powered consultant. Their expertise can be helpful, but it's not necessary.) The larger your congregation or the more conflicted it is, the more important it is to use an outside voice to ask these questions. Get a cross section of the congregation together for an evening of conversation. Ask the questions without qualification. Take the answers at face value. Remember you are simply taking the temperature of the congregational stewardship culture, not prescribing a cure.

After the congregational stewardship culture is assessed, the pastor and leaders must return to the Scriptures and envision what a new stewardship culture would look like. This newly envisioned culture will seek to celebrate and strengthen what is good, right, and salutary in the current culture; remember, not everything needs to be changed. There will also need to be some honest reflection upon what needs to be confessed, absolved, and avoided. Does the congregation need to be better stewards corporately? Is there a need to confess and be more transparent over how stewardship takes place in the congregation? Is there a need to repent of institutional survival and to embrace a much more kingdom of God–oriented stewardship? This is not an exhaustive list. It is merely for starters. Again, it might help to have a consultant, neighboring pastor, or denominational official to help. What is being done here refers back to chapter 2. This step is really putting words to the *why* of stewardship in the local congregation.

Next, the pastor and congregational leaders begin to live out this new culture. Remember, to change the culture, you do not need consensus. Rather, what you need is the move to the tipping point. Shepherds lead; they do not stand in the back of the herd and give orders. Here is where the pastor becomes the chief steward that John Herrmann and Scott Rodin talk about (see chapter 1). This is leading by example. When the sheep know the voice of the Good Shepherd and the faithful under-shepherd to whom he has committed their care, they will follow.

Like Grandma and Grandpa Meador's garden grew from sprout, to leaf, to produce under the skillful and persistent hand of a master gardener, so also will the stewardship culture change start to take shape under the leadership of faithful pastoral care. This shaping takes place when the teaching and preaching of faithful stewardship flows regularly from the pulpit. When the word of God is taught in its truth and purity, a new culture takes shape. This culture is also formed in the stewardship stories that are told. Newsletters, video blog entries, and testimonies are key ways of accomplishing this. When those who have taken up the vision of the new stewardship culture have their stories told, others take up the mantle. Telling these stories doesn't make the good works of the faithful steward the focus. It always points to the faithfulness of God!

Conclusion

Every congregation has a stewardship culture. It is not perfect, but it is not all bad, either. Because culture is about "the way things are done," and the people doing them in the local congregation are sinner-saints, there will always be a need for improvement in the stewardship culture. It will be a process that never arrives at its destination this side of eternity; however, that does not mean it is not an effort that should be undertaken. Pastoral care is what moves us to call God's people to repentance. That is what a pastor is called to do. There are no shortcuts in this process. It takes time. Time is exactly what the Lord has given us.

CHAPTER 5

The Good News of Stewardship

Nathan Meador and Heath R. Curtis

WE HAVE COME FULL CIRCLE IN THIS STEW-ardship journey. We started with the stories of a couple of pastors who have been on quite an adventure in stewardship. Our stories led us into God's story of stewardship. This is the *why* of stewardship. From the pages of the Scriptures, we found that the office of steward was one for which humans were created. Reflecting the will of the Creator within creation, we stewards bear the divine image in the manner in which we manage all of life and life's resources for the glory of God and to benefit our neighbors. While our first parents failed in this task, God did not give up on his stewards. Instead, he redeemed them for the purpose of being stewards of the gospel of Jesus Christ.

From the *why*, we moved to the *how* and *what* of stewardship. This is where the door is opened to seeing stewardship as a matter of pastoral care. Pastors teach and preach the word of God. This word, which is profitable for teaching, rebuking, correcting, and training in righteousness, is the very means by which God grants his stewards purpose and grace. This purpose goes against our nature, which we see in the development of congregational stewardship cultures that are about reflecting the image of the people far more than that of God through the creation. When the *how* of stewardship is disconnected from the *why* of stewardship, this is a serious matter.

What is at stake in stewardship? Nothing short of the gospel itself! As we have mentioned a few times, poor stewardship is not just stinginess or a character flaw. It is idolatry. Unfaithful stewardship flies in the face of the first commandment. When we fear, love, and trust in our ability to manage the good gifts of creation rather than the Creator who has given these gifts, our souls are in jeopardy. It is clear in Exodus 20: God is a jealous God who will not share his place with another.

Because of that divine jealousy, there are consequences: he punishes the sins of the fathers to the third and fourth generations of those who hate him (Exod 20:5). Idolatrous stewards hate God. They despise his place by coveting it, scheming to get it, and reaching out in a false claim of ownership. Stewardship unaddressed is sin unaddressed. As St. Paul reminds us, the wages of sin is death (Rom 6:23).

Because stewardship is this serious, it is incumbent on pastors and congregational leaders to see it as a matter of pastoral care. A faithful pastor who knows that a member of the congregation is catting around on his wife will not hesitate to call the philanderer to repentance. A good undershepherd who notices that a few of the flock entrusted to his care have wandered from regular presence at the Lord's house and table will, like Jesus, leave the ninety-nine in the open field and seek the stray. Sound pastoral care will put the pastor in the home of a shut-in, at the bedside of a sick saint, and at the graveside of a departed sibling in the faith. Every one of these situations exemplifies what comes to mind when pastor and faithful alike think of the term "pastoral care." A pastor who fails to discharge these duties is unfit for the Office of the Holy Ministry and should seek other means of employment!

Not many congregants, however, will consider the pastor's admonishing them to faithful stewardship in the same light. There will be accusations that the pastor or the church is "only after my money." Many old jokes have flown from this mentality. A story is told of two men stranded on a desert island with little to no food, water, or shelter. One of the men frantically scurries hither and yon looking for resources. The other man sits quietly on the beach. After a time, the frantic man turns to the calm man and asks, "Aren't you going to do anything to help?" The second man answers emphatically, "I make over a million dollars a year. I also tithe. My pastor WILL find me!" While that story is intended to be humorous, it is rather sad. It implies that the pastor is more concerned about the hundred thousand dollars than the saint entrusted to his care.

This can only happen when the stewardship culture of a congregation has severed stewardship from its roots in the word and grafted it onto the weed of institutional survival. To be sure, there is a need for the institution of the church. There are important infrastructure and staffing needs that help in the ministry of the gospel. In our twenty-first-century world, that will require a larger and larger financial commitment. As parish pastors, we have families to feed, children to care for and educate, and other necessities, and God uses our salaries to give us what we need to support our lives. Within the church, there are necessities as well, like utilities, comfortable pews, and building maintenance. Just like the temple of old needed support, so does the ministry of the gospel, not only financially but also participatorily. But all that support and participation is intended for the sake of the gospel. The congregation falls into the sin of institutional survival when the survival of the congregation's ministry and the maintaining of the current congregational culture become the end goals. When the operation usurps the prime focus of the congregation assigned by Jesus—to make disciples of all nations by baptizing and teaching everything he has commanded (Matt 28:19)—the gospel suffers. Souls are lost. People within the congregation can allow their idolatrously poor stewardship to separate them from the gospel because they become disenchanted with the institution.

Think about this for a moment. What are some reasons that families might reduce or cease their stewardship support for the congregation? Some that come to mind include the loss of a job, a medical emergency, family discord, or disputes with the pastor about something preached or the direction of the ministry. Which of these in the list is not a matter for pastoral care? A change in stewardship patterns is a key tip-off for the caretaker of souls. If stewardship is simply a matter of institutional survival or the necessities of doing the business of church, souls are lost! In godly stewardship that is built on the solid foundation of the word of God, the work of the gospel is at stake.

YOUR STEWARDSHIP STORY AND YOUR CONGREGATION'S

For the first decades of our ministry, our stewardship stories were rather shallow. We thought we knew something about it. But as we learned, a little knowledge is a dangerous thing. As we look back on the various aspects of how we ended up rewriting our stewardship stories, we feel a sense of repentance and remorse. This starts personally. In retrospect, our own underdeveloped stewardship stories hindered our pastoral care of our people. We both thought we were doing fine; however, the Lord's call to his under-shepherds is not a call to be "fine." It is a call to be faithful. St. Paul reminds pastors that they "are servants of Christ and stewards of the mysteries of God. Moreover, it is required of stewards that they be found trustworthy" (1 Cor 4:1–2). These mysteries are tied directly to the gospel. "Therefore, if anyone is in Christ, he is a new creation. The old has passed away; behold, the new has come. All this is from God, who through Christ reconciled us to himself and gave us the ministry of reconciliation; that is, in Christ God was reconciling the world to himself, not counting their trespasses against them, and entrusting to us the message of reconciliation" (2 Cor 5:17–19). Our stewardship of the mysteries encompasses all of the ministry, including stewardship. To be trustworthy is much more than being "fine" or "good enough." The standard is being faithful. Having an underdeveloped stewardship story stood in the way of our faithfulness.

The same is true of every pastor. Pastors are to be stewards of the mysteries. This includes faithfully and fully forming the stewards entrusted to their care. But the axiom is true: you cannot give away what you do not have. If a pastor does not have a stewardship story formed by the word of God, it will be impossible for him to pass one on to those entrusted to his care. It is critical that pastors learn how to put words to their stewardship *why*. When the pastor as chief steward can clearly articulate a theology of stewardship in his own life, he will be able to cast a vision for stewardship change in the lives of his hearers. This can be a bit of a dangerous thing; it may well make him deal with his own stewardship demons. Perhaps low salaries and rising demands have allowed the pastor to excuse less-than-faithful stewardship. In denominations like ours, which require a master of divinity degree just to start in the parish ministry, the massive student debt that accompanies higher education often hampers both the perception and the reality of what faithful stewardship as a pastor can be. On the other hand, if the pastor is only programmatic in his stewardship, it is possible that putting a biblically faithful stewardship *why* into words may well reveal some self-righteousness. Either way, putting words to the individual stewardship *why* begins with repentance. Confession leads to absolution. Forgiveness, the very heart of the gospel, reconciles us to God. Then, we have committed to us the ministry of reconciliation. This is true in justification and sanctification. That means it is true in stewardship, too.

FAITHFUL STEWARDS IN
AN UNFAITHFUL WORLD

When you know your personal stewardship *why* story, it sets you free to pastorally care for others. This is important for those entrusted to our pastoral care. The people individually and the congregation corporately are carrying the gospel to a totally different world from the one in which we grew up.

While some things I grew up with—Nintendo, Bon Jovi, dial-up internet—have stuck around, come back around, or developed into twenty-first-century versions of themselves, other aspects of our culture have seen more of a break than a development.

When we were born, a solid majority of Americans were Protestant Christians, and the evangelical share of that majority was on the ascendancy. Today, the country is evenly split (at 23 percent) among evangelicals, Catholics, and the "nones" (those with no religious affiliation), while the old mainline denominations languish at around 11 percent.

You have heard these stats, right? The Southern Baptist Convention lost a million members in a decade; the United Methodists decreased by 30 percent in a generation; Roman Catholics lost three million members in just seven years. Less than half (44 percent) of folks who grew up as non-denominational evangelicals remain in those churches as adults. Today, mainstream and conservative news outlets report on these trends regularly.

But nobody saw this coming in 1980. No denomination's national office was planning for this in 1990. And then, all of a sudden, a tipping point was reached, and here we are.

There are bright spots in this data as well. For example, the percentage of Americans who are evangelical Christians *who are very active in the faith* has actually held pretty steady. There is also evidence that religious people are having more children in healthier families than those outside the faith. But those big declines are troubling, and they have obvious implications for churches.

I learned a lot about these demographic trends, and more sociology than I ever thought I would have to as a pastor, after I started my stewardship work with our denomination. Time after time I would hear the same thing after conducting a stewardship workshop with a group of congregational leaders: "Thanks for the info—very helpful. Our giving is decent right now, and this will certainly help. But let me bend your ear about something else. When I think of what our congregation looked like ten years ago, and what it looks like now, with a lot more grey hairs in the pew, I start to wonder about the next ten years."

So the department that we serve in the LCMS hired outside experts to examine the numbers. One of those experts, Professor George Hawley of the University of Alabama, became so interested that he went beyond my own church body and wrote a book called *Demography, Culture, and the Decline of America's Christian Denominations*. Catchy title, eh?

What does all this have to do with your church's stewardship? Think of how the last decade has gone in your congregation and community. Trends being what they are, you will in the next decade probably find things to be a little more challenging. Of course, you might have local reasons for thinking times will be a lot better or a lot worse. It would certainly be a good idea to buy a demographic report for your local area and really study the numbers.

These numbers will help you address the *what* of stewardship more pastorally. But this *what*, if it is to be faithful, can only flow from the *why*. You will certainly need to teach what the Bible says about supporting the mission of the church, ask the people to step out in faith, and plan your church's finances accordingly. This is the golden circle of faithful stewardship in action. Putting words to the congregation's *why* of stewardship will open up a greater understanding of the *how* of stewardship. On average, things look to be more challenging for churches in the next decade. Do you want to face these challenges with your current culture of stewardship? You need to start your stewardship journey in the right place.

Gospel Stewardship

Getting people into the right place in stewardship is at its heart pastoral care. Pastors want those entrusted to their care to know who they are in light of the gospel. What they will find is that stewards are at the same time saints and sinners. They are fully redeemed by the once-for-all sacrifice of Jesus on the cross and restored to their identity as Christian stewards. The mercy of the cross has once again made the life of worshiping stewardship one of joy. This joy can be lived out even if the world in which we stewards live and work is far from the Eden of old or the New Jerusalem of the last day. Fundamentally, we only have one thing to steward. That one thing, the one great trust we have from God to manage for his purposes, is the gospel.

The gospel changes the way we see the relationship between Creator and steward, Redeemer and redeemed. The gospel also changes the way we view the world. Through the gospel, the Holy Spirit causes us to see that the world, the entire cosmos, has been redeemed by Christ (John 3:16). What was once very good is now in the redemptive work of Christ guaranteed to be very good once again for eternity. When the gospel causes us to see creation differently, it also helps us see our neighbors differently. The people around us, especially those who do not know the call to follow Jesus, will have a vastly different view of stewardship, one of either fear or fatalism. The gospel is the only thing that changes this sad situation. It frees from fear and fatalism and opens the eternal door of faith.

Stewardship is all of this. It is much more than budgets, bills, and balance sheets. It is pastoral care. It is the call to teach people who God has made and redeemed them to be. This identity calls them to activity. What stewards do is serve as instruments of God. Changed in their relationship to God by the work of the Holy Spirit in bringing them to faith in Jesus Christ, faithful stewards use created gifts to share the message of the gospel with other lost stewards.

Your stewardship story and the steward-ship story of your congregation are a matter of the gospel. That means it is really not your work. God's Holy Spirit is working in and through you. Repentance, forgiveness, faith, and stewardship are all works of the Spirit. This is what makes stewardship such a wonderful gift of pastoral care. Stewardship, taught in the way of the Scriptures, is not a burden; it is a blessing. To our neighbors. For the kingdom of God. May God bless you as you learn to put the *why* into your stewardship story. It is pastoral care in action.

Acknowledgments

WE WOULD LIKE TO GIVE THANKS TO THE FOL-
lowing people: Harold L. Senkbeil, who has
encouraged us to treat stewardship as a matter of
the care of souls.

The ministry of DOXOLOGY and their executive directors, Dr. Beverly Yahnke and Rev. David
Fleming. It is more than giving!

Rev. Bart Day, Rev. Robert Zagore, and the
staff of the LCMS Office of National Mission, for
their partnership in ministry.

The saints of St. John Lutheran Church in
Plymouth, Wisconsin, for their constant support
and willingness to be the stewards the Lord has
made and redeemed them to be.

The saints of Trinity Lutheran Church in
Worden, Illinois, and Zion Lutheran Church
in Carpenter, Illinois, for their faithful generosity
in imitation of Christ.

Resources

> Alcorn, Randy. *The Treasure Principle: Unlocking the Secret of Joyful Giving.* Multnomah, 2017.

This book is based on Jesus' comment in the Sermon on the Mount: "For where your treasure is, there your heart will be also" (Matt 6:21). Alcorn builds a biblical vision for generosity and stewardship from this simple concept: your heart always goes where you put God's money.

> Curtis, Heath. *Stewardship Under the Cross: Stewardship for the Confessional Lutheran Parish.* 2nd ed. Lulu, 2013.

Pastor Curtis narrates his congregation's journey through its first financial crunch. He includes a lot of detail on specific resources, Bible studies, and timelines that were used over the course of that first year of stewardship education.

> Lane, Charles R. *Ask, Thank, Tell: Improving Stewardship Ministry in Your Congregation*. Augsburg, 2006.

Lane walks the reader through a transformation in stewardship thinking. He believes the foundation of stewardship is in discipleship. Starting from this sound theological basis, he moves to introducing a framework for raising up stewards and freeing stewardship from the captivity of "paying the bills."

> Miller, Herb. *New Consecration Sunday*. Abingdon, 1993.

Miller provides a simple, but not simplistic, programmatic approach to introducing a congregation to the concept of practicing faithful stewardship. This is simply the best place to start for a congregation of any size that is at a dead stop in stewardship ministry. It serves as a jumpstart that will lay the groundwork for the necessary stewardship transformation.

> Nepos, Cornelius. *Lives of the Great Commanders*. Translated by Quintus Curtius. Fortress of the Mind, 2019.

This book isn't Christian at all; it's by a pagan who lived at the time of Julius Caesar. And so it's perhaps the most interesting in expanding our understanding of the role that generosity plays in the formation of leaders and how they should demonstrate generosity to those they lead.

> Rodin, R. Scott. *Stewards in the Kingdom: A Theology of Life in All Its Fullness.* IVP Academic, 2009.

This is a must-read for pastors seeking a better understanding of stewardship from a theological perspective. Rodin's connection of stewardship to practical theology lays the groundwork for "docking the ship" and starting to talk about stewards and their call to be who God has created and redeemed them to be.

> Sinek, Simon. *Start with Why: How Great Leaders Inspire Everyone to Take Action.* Portfolio, 2011.

This is *not* a theology book. It is a great book for helping steward leaders focus their leadership and vision for service. Putting words to the *why* helps those in leadership help those who follow them to a deeper commitment. This is a helpful way to start the transition from seeing stewardship as an activity (*what* and *how*) to seeing the true identity of stewards from creation and baptism.

> ➢ Sitze, Bob. *Stewardshift: An Economia for Congregational Change*. Morehouse, 2016.

This book is a bit edgier than the others, but it challenges the reader to take a fresh look at stewardship. It's helpful for those who wish to deepen their biblical understanding of the need to rightly view the steward's identity and purpose.

> ➢ Willmer, Wesley K. *God and Your Stuff: The Vital Connection between Your Possessions and Your Soul*. NavPress, 2002.

A direct, in-your-face call for congregational repentance when it comes to the teaching of stewardship. Willmer boldly makes the connection between failed stewardship and idolatry. It is a great read for a stewardship leader or committee to get motivated to start the process of changing the stewardship culture of their congregation.

Notes

1. The LCMS is made up of over 6,100 congregations. Its national headquarters are in St. Louis, Missouri. For governance and structure, it is divided into thirty-five mostly geographic districts. Each district provides resources and support for the ministry of local congregations.

2. John Herrmann was the director of stewardship for the LCMS in the early 1950s. His work published in 1951 (and now out of print) is still regarded as the gold standard of stewardship writing in the LCMS. Its early chapters provide a wonderful exposition of the role of the pastor in leading the congregation in stewardship. The final chapters, though dated, are an interesting read for understanding leadership in a previous era.

3. Simon Sinek, *Start with Why* (Penguin, 2009), 39. For a brief introduction to Sinek's thinking, see his TED talk, "How Great Leaders Inspire Action," www.ted.com/talks/simon_sinek_how_great_leaders_inspire_action.

4. Sinek, *Start with Why*, 56.

5. Sinek, *Start with Why*, 57.

6. LCMS Stewardship Ministry, LCMS.org/stewardship.

7. The Hebrew word is *tselem*. Victor Hamilton, *The Book of Genesis Chapters 1-17* (Eerdmans, 2004), 137

8. Claus Westermann, *Genesis 1-11: A Continental Commentary* (Augsburg, 1984), 220.

9. Patrick Lai, "Avodah: Work is Worship," *Business for Transformation* (blog), March 31, 2014, https://b4tblog.com/avodah-work-is-worship/.

10. R. Scott Rodin, *Steward Leader: Transforming People, Organizations and Communities* (IVP Academic, 2010), 38.

11. Kenneth Korby, "The Church at Worship," in *The Lively Function of the Gospel*, ed. Robert Bertram (Concordia, 1966), 60.

12. For example, according to Nonprofits Source, only 10–25 percent of the members of a typical American congregation tithe, and Americans give just 2.5 percent of their income to churches (nonprofitssource.com/online-giving-statistics).

13. We often forget that the Bible gives the chief role in teaching to *parents* (Deut 6; Eph 6). If you aren't teaching the parents how to teach their children, then two groups of people are being cheated!

14. We could draw one more larger circle: folks on the membership list who are not active in worship. But for the purposes of changing the culture of a congregation, those folks will quite literally remain on the periphery. They might check the

Facebook page or get a monthly newsletter in the mail, but so long as they are absent from the worshiping body of Christ, they are in the truest sense outside the fellowship of the congregation.

15. Chris Willard and Jim Sheppard, *Contagious Generosity: Creating a Culture of Giving in Your Church* (Zondervan, 2012), 29.

16. Willard and Sheppard, *Contagious Generosity*, 42.

17. Wesley K. Willmer, ed., *Revolution in Generosity: Transforming Stewards to be Rich toward God* (Moody, 2008), 119.

18. C. K. Robertson, *Transforming Stewardship* (Church, 2009), 14.

Works Cited

Hamilton, Victor. *The Book of Genesis Chapters 1–17.* Eerdmans, 2004.

Korby, Kenneth. "The Church at Worship." In *The Lively Function of the Gospel,* ed. Robert Bertram, 60. Concordia, 1966.

Lai, Patrick. "Avodah: Work is Worship." *Business for Transformation* (blog), March 31, 2014. https://b4tblog.com/avodah-work-is-worship/.

Matthews, Kenneth. *Genesis 1:1–11:26.* New American Commentary. Broadman & Holman, 1996.

Robertson, C. K. *Transforming Stewardship.* Church, 2009.

Rodin, R. Scott. *Steward Leader: Transforming People, Organizations and Communities.* IVP Academic, 2010.

Sinek, Simon. *Start with Why: How Great Leaders Inspire Everyone to Take Action.* Portfolio, 2011.

Westermann, Claus. *Genesis 1–11: A Continental Commentary*. Augsburg, 1984.

Willard, Chris, and Jim Sheppard. *Contagious Generosity: Creating a Culture of Giving in Your Church*. Zondervan, 2012.

Willmer, Wesley K. *Revolution in Generosity: Transforming Stewards to be Rich toward God*. Moody, 2008.

—

PASTORS CARE FOR A SOUL IN THE WAY A DOCTOR CARES FOR A BODY.

In a time when many churches have lost sight of the real purpose of the church, *The Care of Souls* invites a new generation of pastors to form the godly habits and practical wisdom needed to minister to the hearts and souls of those committed to their care.

"Pastoral theology at its best. Every pastor, and everyone who wants to be a pastor, should read this book."
—Timothy George, Founding Dean, Beeson Divinity School, Samford University; General Editor, Reformation Commentary on Scripture